FRANCIS FRITH'S

TOWN & CITY

MEMORIES

KETTERING

THE MARKET PLACE 1922 72232

FRANCIS FRITH'S
TOWN & CITY
MEMORIES

KETTERING

MALPAS PEARSE

FRANCIS FRITH'S
TOWN & CITY
MEMORIES

First published as Kettering, A Photographic History of your Town
in 2002 by Black Horse Books, an imprint of The Francis Frith Collection
Revised edition published in the United Kingdom in 2005 by
The Francis Frith Collection as Kettering, Town and City Memories
Limited Hardback Edition ISBN 1-84589-070-1
Paperback Edition ISBN 1-84589-038-8

British Library Cataloguing in Publication Data

Kettering
Town and City Memories
Malpas Pearse

The Francis Frith Collection®
Frith's Barn, Teffont,
Salisbury, Wiltshire SP3 5QP
Tel: +44 (0) 1722 716 376
Email: info@francisfrith.co.uk
www.francisfrith.co.uk

Aerial photographs reproduced under licence from Simmons Aerofilms Limited
Historical Ordnance Survey maps reproduced under licence from Homecheck.co.uk

Printed and bound in England

Front Cover: **KETTERING, THE MARKET 1922** 72232t
The colour-tinting in this image is for illustrative purposes only,
and is not intended to be historically accurate

FRANCIS FRITH'S
TOWN & CITY
MEMORIES

CONTENTS

The Making of an Archive

F rancis Frith, Victorian founder of the world-famous photographic archive, was a devout Quaker and a highly successful Victorian businessman. By 1860 he was already a multi-millionaire, having established and sold a wholesale grocery business in Liverpool. He had also made a series of pioneering photographic journeys to the Nile region. The images he returned with were the talk of London. An eminent modern historian has likened their impact on the population of the time to that on our own generation of the first photographs taken on the surface of the moon.

Frith had a passion for landscape, and was as equally inspired by the countryside of Britain as he was by the desert regions of the Nile. He resolved to set out on a new career and to use his skills with a camera. He established a business in Reigate as a specialist publisher of topographical photographs.

Frith lived in an era of immense and sometimes violent change. For the poor in the early part of Victoria's reign work was a drudge and the hours long, and ordinary people had precious little free time. Most had not travelled far beyond the boundaries of their own town or village. Mass tourism was in its infancy during the 1860s, but during the next decade the railway network and the establishment of Bank Holidays and half-Saturdays gradually made it possible for the working man and his family to enjoy holidays and to see a little more of the world. With characteristic business acumen, Francis Frith foresaw that these new tourists would enjoy having souvenirs to commemorate their days out. He began selling photo-souvenirs of seaside resorts and beauty spots, which the Victorian public pasted into treasured family albums.

Frith's aim was to photograph every town and village in Britain. For the next thirty years he travelled the country by train and by pony and trap, producing fine photographs of seaside resorts and beauty spots that were keenly bought by millions of Victorians.

The Rise of Frith & Co

Each photograph was taken with tourism in mind, the small team of Frith photographers concentrating on busy shopping streets, beaches, seafronts, picturesque lanes and villages. They also photographed buildings: the Victorian and Edwardian eras were times of huge building activity, and town halls, libraries, post offices, schools and technical colleges were springing up all over the country. They were invariably celebrated by a proud Victorian public, and photo souvenirs – visual records – published by F Frith & Co were sold in their hundreds of thousands. In addition, many new commercial buildings such as hotels, inns and pubs were photographed, often because their owners specifically commissioned Frith postcards or prints of them for re-sale or for publicity purposes.

In order to gain some understanding of the scale of Frith's business one only has to look at the catalogue issued by Frith & Co in 1886: it runs to some 670 pages. By 1890 Frith had created the greatest specialist photographic publishing company in the world, with over 2,000 stockists! The picture on the right shows the Frith & Co display board on the wall of the stockist at Ingleton in the Yorkshire Dales (left of window). Beautifully constructed with a mahogany frame and gilt inserts, it displayed a dozen scenes.

Postcard Bonanza

The ever-popular holiday postcard we know today took many years to appear, and F Frith & Co was in the vanguard of its development. Postcards became a hugely popular means of communication and sold in their millions. Frith's company took full advantage of this boom and soon became the major publisher of photographic view postcards.

Francis Frith died in 1898 at his villa in Cannes, his great project still growing. His sons Eustace and Cyril continued their father's monumental task, expanding the number of views offered to the public and recording more and more places in Britain, as the coasts and countryside were opened up to mass travel. The archive Frith created continued in business for another seventy years. By 1970 it contained over a third of a million pictures of 7,000 cities, towns and villages. The massive photographic record Frith has left to us stands as a living monument to a special and very remarkable man.

This book shows Kettering as it was photographed by this world-famous archive at various periods in its development over the past 150 years. Every photograph was taken for a specific commercial purpose, which explains why the selection may not show every aspect of the town landscape. However, the photographs, compiled from one of the world's most celebrated archives, provide an important and absorbing record of your town.

APPROACHES

If you half close your eyes and frame a picture of Kettering from the Northampton Road (the A43), it still has the charm of a 19th-century market town. The parish church dominates the landscape, framed in a collar of trees (72245, opposite). However, the rural lane has become a busy road which is now bisected by the A14, a roaring motorway which links the east coast with the centre of England.

Transport has revolutionised Kettering for a second time in its history. The first revolution had been caused by the railway. Kettering had been a market town with a small weaving industry; but by the late 19th century it had become a manufacturing centre for boots and shoes. With rail transport the town began to export footwear to the rest of the world. It grew into a web of terraced streets in clusters round factories modelled on baronial halls and Venetian palaces; and there was also a proliferation of chapels. However, nothing has been as disturbing as wayward planning in the past 50 years, which has resulted in the demolition of much of the old town centre.

Kettering originated in pre-Anglo-Saxon England when it was one of a string of settlements along the Nene Valley, all well-drained but with access to water, and so easily cultivated. During the 10th century the East Midlands were ruled through strata of ealdermen or earls; beneath them the lords of the manors controlled their smaller estates. 'Cytringan' was a gift to Elfsige from Edwy in 956. When King Edgar ruled, there was a royal disposition to donate land to the church, and 'Kyteringan' was given to the monks of Medeshamstede, under the diocese of Peterborough. When Edgar died in 975, freebooters moved in and snatched back the lands which had been given to the church. Leofsige grabbed Peterborough, Oundle and Kettering. He held them for two years while the whole country was in a period of uncertainty and fields were uncultivated. When Edward the Confessor became king, he reclaimed land for the church. The monks still owned 'Cateringe' in 1086, according to the Domesday Book.

By 1227, Kettering had become large enough for Henry III to grant a charter for a weekly market on Fridays, and a 'Feast' to be held for seven days in June. They still take place, and a fair visits the town annually. The fairground is on the edge of the Northampton Road, still pastoral in the photograph (72245, right); even now the celebration is held on land which has been used for field sports for generations.

This rural lane leading to Kettering was to change dramatically in the 1930s, when it would be bordered by large detached houses with elaborate gardens. The railway bridge is now too low for tall lorries, which are diverted. To the right, obscured by the trees, is the railway station.

Approaches

Until 50 years ago, it was not unusual for towns to become associated with one product: Axminster made carpets, for instance, and Stoke made china. The Northamptonshire towns teemed with shoe factories and all the trades associated with them: lasts, heels, laces and machinery were made in workshops in the towns. From 1850 until 1950, leather was Kettering's business; but when cheaper foreign imports flooded the market, the footwear factories closed. In 1934 there were 29 shoe manufacturers and over 30 workshops connected with leather. Now there is only a handful of businesses associated with shoemaking. Those factories which have not been pulled down have been turned into apartment blocks. The sites have become new housing developments or supermarkets.

Quarrying was another local occupation, producing iron ore from open cast mines in nearby villages and on the outskirts of town. Three-foot-gauge railways threaded the area, carrying ore to blast furnaces situated between the railway and Rockingham Road. The furnaces were worked between 1878 and 1954, and although Kettering people became accustomed to the red glow in the sky all night and all day, it became a special landmark for rail passengers travelling past at night. The quarry sites were filled in after their usefulness was over: some became farmland, others were used for housing developments.

NONCONFORMITY

Before the shoemakers, weavers were the mainstay of Kettering. They worked in their own homes before factories existed. There was a tradition of stubborn radicalism in the weaving trade, which would continue in the boot and shoe industry. This anti-establishment attitude was manifest as early as 1666. The 'Great Meeting' was formed by John Maidwell, who was then the rector of the parish church. When Charles II had returned six years earlier, he brought back the Church of England. Kettering was obviously still loyal to the Puritan religion, and Maidwell preferred to leave the safety of his church to form his own chapel in Hazelwood Lane. 20 years later, there was another breakaway when the 'Little Meeting' set up a Baptist chapel in Gold Street.

On 2 October 1792 a group of local Baptist ministers met in Widow Wallis's house in Lower Street and formed the Baptist Missionary Society, collecting £13.2.6 in Andrew Fuller's snuffbox to launch the movement, which disseminated medicine and education as well as religion. While Fuller stayed in the town and organised the society, two missionaries from Kettering set off to make real changes. William Carey went to India; here his family suffered, while he managed to translate the bible into Bengali and founded the Agro-Horticultural Society of India in 1830.

William Knibb was another Baptist missionary; he went to Kingston, Jamaica. He was aghast at the realities of slavery, and worked for emancipation. After imprisonment he returned to England, where he continued to campaign until the abolition of slavery in 1833. It was estimated that 300,000 slaves were liberated by his efforts. A strong nonconformist and Liberal tradition was to remain in Kettering, along with a sense of local identity and civic pride.

MANOR HOUSE GARDENS 1922 72246

This quiet enclave of art gallery, library and
Manor House flanks the church. Out of sight to
the right is the Grammar School of 1913, now
the offices of the Borough Council.

Climbing the hill by the Northampton Road, we arrive at an area which Pevsner called 'an effort towards a Civic Centre' when he compiled 'Northamptonshire' in 1961. Just before the crest of the hill there is a junction of five roads. We will be exploring towards the north, where the town centre was built in a myriad of small lanes converging upon three or four streets. Immediately in front, moving towards the crest of the hill, are the Manor House Gardens, and the Alfred East Art Gallery (72246, above). As we enter the gardens and look back down the hill, we can see the arrowhead convergence of Northampton Road and Station Road (72236, page 12) behind us.

When the railway station was opened in 1857, it also opened the way to mass production: the boot and shoe industry took off with the trains. Thomas Gotch set up as a shoemaker and leather dresser in 1786. His home-working enterprise grew to a big business employing many out-workers as he fulfilled army contracts during the Napoleonic wars. He ran the business from Chesham House in Lower Street. This elegant building of 1762 is still standing, although it is now in a car park. Gotch also founded a bank. He had one son, John Cooper Gotch, who ran the bank and the shoe industry until the fateful day in 1857 when the bank folded. However, with the advent of the rail link south to London, the shoemakers who had been trained

SHEEP STREET

by the Gotches set up their own workshops, and then factories, throughout Kettering.

Station Road (72236, right) often seemed like a scene from a rodeo until the central cattle market in the town closed in 1967. The market was behind the Manor House and the Grammar School (now the Borough Council offices), and livestock was herded through the streets to be loaded onto cattle trucks at the station. On the downhill slope of Station Road they would break into a run, and pedestrians rushed into strangers' gardens and barricaded themselves behind gates and hedges to escape the stampede.

As manufacturers became more involved with offices in London, they built homes within easy reach of the station. Most of the remaining houses in Station Road (72236) have been turned into offices, and some have been replaced by modern flats, but in Queensberry Road and The Headlands there are still comfortable late Victorian villas which are relics of Kettering's 19th-century prosperity.

Glancing back down the hill from the Manor House Gardens (K13032, pages 14-15), it is also possible to see a short row of almshouses wedged on a busy corner of the road junction between a garage and the traffic lights. Edmund Sawyer must have been a swashbuckling adventurer. He left his family home at Kettering Manor and became a merchant at Aleppo in Syria. He left £600 in 1687 for the relief of the poor of his home town. His sister Joyce had six almshouses built with the legacy. They were turned into three

STATION ROAD 1922 72236

Large late Victorian houses lined Station Road, the adjacent Queensberry Road and the Headlands, built for businessmen who 'commuted' to London.

SHEEP STREET

MANOR HOUSE GARDENS c1955 K13032

This photograph shows the busy junction at the top of Station Road and Northampton Road, which combine like an arrowhead opposite the Gardens. The Headlands stretches off to the left. Sawyers Almshouses can be seen through the trees to the right.

The Alfred East Gallery (72244, page 17) at the entrance to Sheep Street looks like an outsize tomb, so it is appropriate that soon after the gallery had been opened in 1913, Sir Alfred should lie there in state like a king while Kettering people filed past him. The gallery had been built to house a collection of paintings he was to leave to the town; how uncanny that he should become one of the first exhibits!

At the end of the 19th century, he was an establishment artist — he was an associate of the Royal Academy and President of the Royal Society of British Artists. Yet he had wild moments too: Alfred East spent summers in Cornwall, usually in St Ives, or visiting another well-known Kettering painter, Thomas Gotch, who lived and worked in Newlyn. They were part of that unconventional mildly Bohemian circle that included Stanhope Forbes, Laura Knight, and occasionally Augustus John. Their loose vigorous paintings in sunlit colours attempted to bring the brilliance of French Impressionism into England.

Like many Kettering buildings, the gallery was designed by Gotch and Saunders. J A Gotch was the brother of Thomas Cooper Gotch, the painter; his other two brothers stayed in the boot and shoe business. They were closely involved with the growth of education in the town, and a comprehensive school is named after Henry Gotch. Because one firm of architects was pre-eminent in Kettering from the 1890s until the 1930s, the town developed in a pleasantly uniform way. J A Gotch was an expert on Elizabethan and Jacobean buildings, and he was also interested in old building materials and techniques. Gotch and Saunders were responsible for much of Kettering's architecture, which is often brick-built with stone facings round the windows and doors. It is solid, unassuming and timeless.

The library (K13108, page 18), which opened in 1904, is attached to the art gallery corridor. Its low-built shape set the style for Piccadilly Buildings, a parade of shops facing the library (K13045, page 16, and K13033 on pages 18-19). This replaced stabling for the George Hotel in 1924 (72237, pages 16-17). Close to the cattle market, the George was a popular farmers' 'ordinary'. Originally called the Cock, the name was probably changed in a fit of patriotic fervour in the 18th century. In 1896 it was advertised as having 'ten loose boxes, a five stall, a four stall and two stall stables, two coach houses, a cow house for eight

SHEEP STREET

cows, a large yard and a pig yard'. Behind the façade of the shops the car park of the hotel has supplanted the stockyard.

There are two monuments in Sheep Street. A bronze bust of Sir Alfred East rules over a tiny garden set between the gallery and the library, just visible in 72244 (page 17). Nearby, on the pavement edge, is the Dryland Memorial.

Kettering owed much to its doctors. Doctor Dryland was instrumental in forming the Local Government Board in 1872. This was a precursor to the Urban Council, which in turn became the Borough Council. Dryland worked hard for a more hygenic town, and especially for a pure water supply, so it is fitting that he is remembered by a horse trough and drinking fountain — even if they are now empty.

The Manor House was still called the Abbot's House in the early 18th century. It may have been preceded by the monastic buildings from which Kettering grew. The Manor House is hidden from Sheep Street by the library and a small brick building which houses the Tourist Information Office. Largely Georgian, the manor is now the town museum. Part of the charm of this part of Kettering is a mesh of linking footpaths running around the Manor House, the church and Market Place.

Left: SHEEP STREET c1955 K13045

A 'new style' double-decker bus pulls up at the Library bus stop. Piccadilly Buildings, opposite, were designed to harmonise with the Library. This parade of select shops on the left included Coles, selling ladies' dresses, and an off-licence — the Hotel Vaults. A small café catered for those who arrived early for the bus, and who needed to rest their baskets and their feet. The zebra crossing was removed later.

SHEEP STREET 1922 72237

This busy junction, uniting five roads, including Northampton Road and Sheep Street, was lit by a single, central lamp post. The house with tall chimneys on the left was the gable-end of the George Hotel, with garaging attached to the main building; the higher gable with the BP sign marks the entrance to the car park. The hotel faces the Market Place and the church. George Street, beyond, which is hidden by buildings, ran from the Market Place towards Dr Roughton's house. In 1933 this land would be sold and was turned into the bus depot.

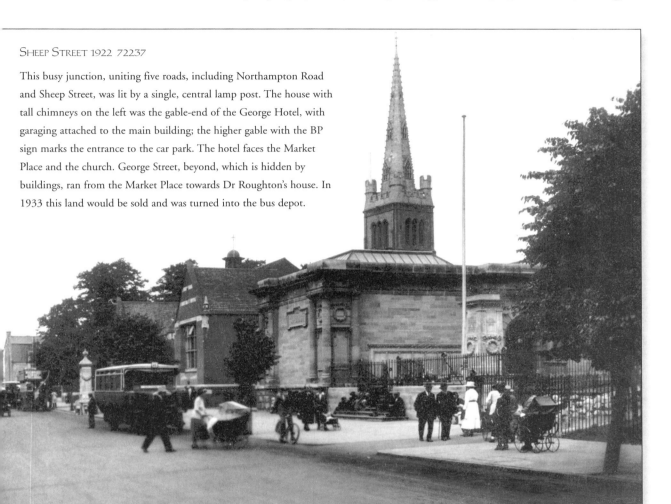

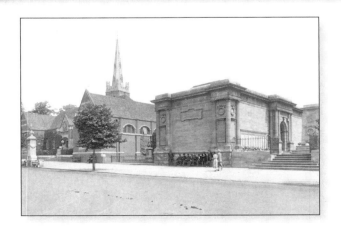

SHEEP STREET, THE LIBRARY AND THE ALFRED EAST GALLERY 1922 72244

In this view, the horse and dog troughs are still attached to the Dryland Memorial, and a row of sitters is taking advantage of the shade. The war memorial is on the extreme right. Above the doorway to the Gallery is the simple inscription LABORE ET AMORE — Work and Love.

SHEEP STREET

Main Picture: SHEEP STREET c1955 K13033

This view of busy Sheep Street shows patient bus
passengers corralled into queues by solid metal barriers.
On the left the parade of Piccadilly Buildings ends
with the George Hotel. The half-timbered building,
on the other side of George Street, is the Cherry Tree
pub. When coaches started from the George the parcels
would be passed to the coachman through the first
floor windows. Further along is a newsagents where
Picture Post and Farmers' Weekly are advertised. Next
door was the Market Tavern.

Right: SHEEP STREET, THE LIBRARY c1965 K13108

A public library had been opened in 1896 in the Corn
Exchange in the Market Place. It then moved to Silver
Street, and finally came to rest here in 1904. The low
brick building, with Ketton stone facings, cost £8,000.
This was given by the philanthropist Andrew Carnegie
(1835-1919), who donated part of his American
fortune to building libraries in the United Kingdom in
memory of what he had learnt in his Scottish youth.
The building is surprisingly unpompous for the period
and looks more like an affluent private house, or a
village school, than a civic building.

SHEEP STREET c1955 K13034

One of the older United Counties single-deckers parks outside the library. During one year there would be other changes; a zebra crossing was later removed, and the older lamp posts with wrought iron branches would be discarded in favour of tall concrete poles. The drinking troughs had been moved from the Dryland Memorial — the white pillar outside the library. They would be re-instated later.

SHEEP STREET

Left: THE BUS STATION C1965 K13079

Until the 1960s, most people relied on public transport, and the green-liveried buses of United Counties carried workers and shoppers in and out of town on busy timetables. Coach tours became very popular, especially to Skegness ('Skeggy') or Hunstanton ('Hunston') - usually on Sundays. They would leave at 7.30am and often would not return until 10.30pm. This is the view from Northampton Road, with the George Hotel roof visible behind the bus station.

Below: SHEEP STREET, THE WAR MEMORIAL 1922 72242

Placed beside the Alfred East Gallery, the memorial faces Northampton Road, still tree-lined in 1922. The names of the fallen are on plaques built into the gallery wall to the right of the obelisk, which simply states: 'Their name liveth for evermore'. Between the memorial and the gallery the end of the George Hotel is visible. This became Piccadilly Buildings in 1924.

THE PARISH CHURCH

D edicated to St Peter and St Paul, the church is recessed from the road and approached by an avenue of trees. The photograph of 1922 shows a row of buildings alongside this driveway (72239, page 23), which would later be demolished. It is easier to appreciate the church tower and spire, now that it is simply garlanded by trees. At 179 feet, this is one of the tallest church spires in Northamptonshire. When Pevsner recorded it, he thought it had 'a curious, ungenuine look, as if it were an imitation, or re-erected'. The tower and the church are Perpendicular (1450-1480), though there are some earlier, 14th-century relics. Most of the windows are clear glass, but in the south chancel aisle there is a window formed from broken pieces of stained glass, which were dug up in the grounds.

The few other stained glass windows include depictions of Saints Crispin and Crispianus, the patron saints of shoemakers, made in

1963; a large window showing scenes from the life of Our Lady was installed when the Lady Chapel was restored in 1927.

At the west end of the north aisle there is a moving memorial of the Second World War. The United States Airforce had a base at nearby Grafton Underwood. On their return from forays over Germany, the pilots used the high spire of Kettering church as a landmark on their way home. The statue of St Christopher was their gift to the church. There are three medieval wall paintings. The one of St Roch is indecipherable; but high on the walls of the clerestory, above the nave, there are some very faded relics of coloured angels. The church has a peal of twelve bells, one of the largest in the county.

A tree-lined avenue leads from the church into Sheep Street, where the Roughton Memorial Gates, another memorial to doctors, would be erected in 1963 (K13080, page 25). The Roughton family lived in the area from 1487 to 1933. Dr William Roughton joined a local

THE PARISH CHURCH

Opposite: THE CHURCH c1960 K13047

This village-like landscape is a reminder of the old centre of Kettering, which clustered around the Manor House and the church. There are now only a few gravestones left in the re-organised area. A garden of rest has covered most of the old churchyard.

Left: THE PARISH CHURCH
AND MEMORIAL CROSS 1922 72239

The Perpendicular tower is 179 feet high, with a battlemented spire. There are four stages with the upper, bell stage, having three openings. The church underwent some restoration in the 19th century, but the basic tall, elegant structure is largely unaltered. The buildings to the right of the gateway, which led in from the Market Place, were part of the District Council offices.

Below: THE PARISH CHURCH OF SAINT PETER
AND SAINT PAUL 1922 72240

There are a few traces left from the early 14th century, but the main parts of the church are Perpendicular, from the second half of the 15th century. The west window was installed in 1893. The large clear windows give the church a light, open atmosphere. The amazing tall tower was probably built before the nave, as buttresses appear inside the building.

practice in 1738, and five generations of doctors succeeded him. The fourth Dr Roughton set up the general hospital, which opened in 1891. He lived behind the George Hotel in a house with gardens stretching beside the (then) rural Northampton Road, where he had a cricket field on which W G Grace played. He commissioned a car from a local maker, Charles Robinson, in 1907. It had an interesting specification: a two-seater, DB983 had an extra large tool-box built across the back, which also held the doctor's medical kit. The box was designed to be used as an emergency operating table. The Robinson car is now in the Manor House museum.

When the fifth Dr Roughton died in 1933, his house and garden were bought by the United Counties bus company. The resulting bus depot had an exit into Sheep Street and the Northampton Road (K13079, page 20).

The Parish Church

Above: The Roman Catholic Church c1965 K13071

St Edward's was completed in 1940, although the redbrick geometrical design looks post-war. Fronting London Road, it faces the entrance to St Mary's Road where the Technical College was to be built in 1955. The houses on the right, examples of the late Victorian baronial style, are an interesting contrast. It is thought that their stone came from buildings in Gold Street which were demolished in 1887.

Right: The Parish Church c1960 K13080

From Sheep Street the driveway to a tier of wide steps approaches the church. The Roughton Memorial gates are decorated with a coat of arms on the left-hand pillar and a brief history of the family's connection with Kettering on the right-hand pillar.

THE MARKET PLACE 1922 72232

Until the 1930s the south side of the market, facing the camera, was bordered by a row of buildings which would be later demolished. The gabled stone building (in front of the church) housed the Market Offices, and was also a drop-in centre for the unemployed. It was built of stone from the Session House, which had stood in the market until 1805. Paynes the bakers were in the pale upright building with advertisements for wedding cakes on the frontage. They were the first commercial ice-cream makers in Kettering. The Albion Temperance Hotel is nearest the road. When this block was demolished it was replaced by a car park.

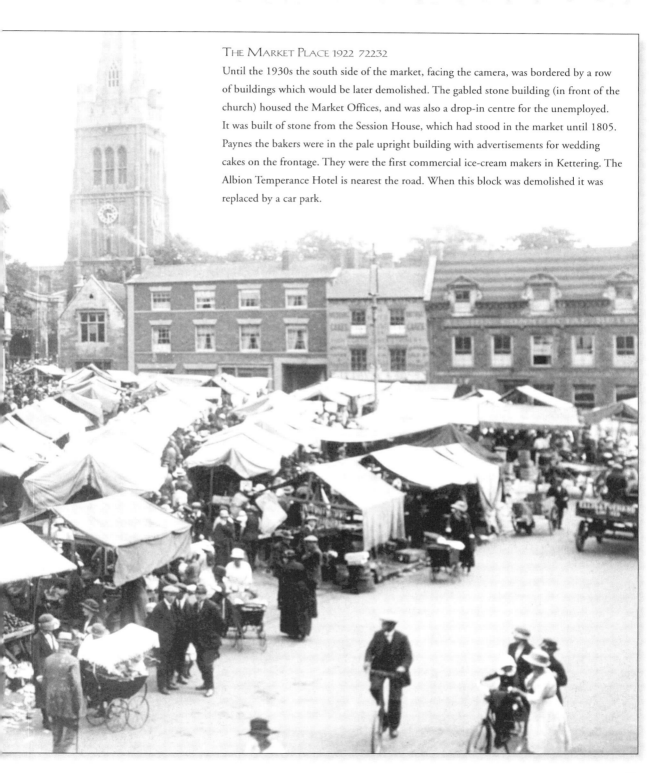

THE MARKET PLACE

The market place, a long triangle in shape, is still on the site of the first charter market; there have been fewer changes here than in other parts of Kettering (72233, opposite). The greatest alteration was the demolition of the terrace at the south end, facing us in the 1922 view (72232, pages 26-27); it was pulled down between 1936 and 1938. The Albion Hotel (72232), the YWCA and a few small shops had been a familiar boundary to the market, but some of the buildings had become very derelict. Although attempts have been made to revive the market's popularity, it has declined in recent years.

The Corn Exchange is a handsome building of 1854. When it was built, by public subscription, the Town Hall was upstairs behind the arched windows, with a lofty view over what was then the busiest part of Kettering. The balcony was used by speakers to address outdoor meetings. It was from his window in the nearby White Hart (later the Royal Hotel, 72233, centre left) that the young journalist Charles Dickens watched a meeting of radical weavers in the 1830s. He was angered by the local farmers and landowners riding their horses into the crowd, lashing at the protesters' faces with their boots and iron stirrups.

The Corn Exchange (the tall building left of the church in 72232) became the Palace cinema and theatre in the early 1900s after a short spell as lending library. The Palace was owned by John Covington, who tried to combine both functions in the days of silent films by placing an actor and actress behind a curtain to read accompanying dialogue. In 1922, the building was sold and re-named the Hippodrome, presenting a continuous performance from 6.15pm to 10.30pm. On Saturday afternoons there was a children's matinee, when there were uproarious fights between the circle and the stalls. The building later became a billiards hall. The parish rooms, between the Corn Exchange and the church, were originally a school for older girls. On the left side of the corn exchange-cum-cinema is a long building with a varied history. At one time it was a dentist's, which in 1913 had an ostentatious placard offering 'English and American Teeth'.

Although there are some new shop fronts on the west side of the market, the upper storeys are largely reminders of Georgian and Victorian Kettering. The Market Tavern was once the Saracen's Head, and was re-named the New Inn in 1815. Looking back at

the market from the High Street (K13026, page 30-31), narrow West Street is flanked by the Royal Hotel and a shop which was the newsagent and tobacconist, Pooles. This unassuming building was once the premises of the ill-fated Gotch Bank which closed so abruptly in 1857. John Cooper Gotch was then probably the most influential man in the town, not only as a shoe manufacturer but also as a leading Liberal and Nonconformist. In 1844 he had arranged a visit to the town by Queen Victoria, who stayed briefly in Room

THE MARKET PLACE
1922 72233

This view from the middle of the Market Place is not much altered since 1922. The view towards the Royal Hotel and Lloyds Bank is almost unchanged. On the right the Victorian Corn Exchange has become the Variety cinema. The fusion of industry and shopping was usual in the town. Baker & Son, boot manufacturers, have their headquarters next to Pears & Sons, the dentists. The stalls were provided by the stall holders until the 1930s, when uniform stalls were supplied by the Borough Council.

12 at the White Hart, which was to be re-named the Royal Hotel in her honour. West Street is a narrow cobbled lane leading to the hotel stables, now the car park. Alongside, another narrow alley went to Hazelwood House, where John Maidwell gathered his first Nonconformist congregation in 1666. The building was demolished in 1955 when it had become derelict.

This was to become the banking area of the town, perhaps because the Market Place once housed the cattle market. The Royal Hotel (72227, pages 34-35) had also gained a grand clientele in the late 19th century when the politically powerful Duke of Buccleuch, who lived at nearby Boughton House, bought the building to turn it into the local Conservative Party headquarters. In 1878, it was virtually rebuilt in the style of Kirby Hall, a great Elizabethan country house in the area. There were later reminders of the Victorian age, however: a magnificent billiards room with a stained glass roof, and ceramic name plates for the bars, were added

after the duke had sold the premises to Pickering, Phipps, a Northampton brewery, in 1896. At this time a bill records that dinner for three people cost 7s 6d (35p). The billiards room has survived; but the public bar with engraved glass windows was pulled down in 1983, in spite of protests by the Civic Society.

The progress of Boots, the nation-wide chemists, charts the movement of popular shopping centres in Kettering. In 1894, the town was considered important enough to deserve a branch. Then, the prime position was opposite the Royal, on the edge of the market place and at the bottom of Market Street (K13026, left). This is an uphill dog-leg-shaped lane leading to the Horsemarket, where a baronial-style Liberal Club demonstrated the distribution of political power in the town. Market Street had several busy pubs, and the entrance to Timpson's shoe factory.

A pedestrian precinct now covers the old streets in the centre of Kettering. It begins at the Royal Hotel, and continues through the High Street and Gold Street as well as Lower Street.

THE MARKET PLACE c1950 K13026

Market stalls were supposed to be erected and removed either side of market days, but inevitably it became easier to leave them stacked for use (left). A pavement ran along the front of the stalls, as earlier markets had strayed into the road. Boots the chemist had built their original store on the corner opposite the Royal Hotel at the bottom of Market Street. Pooles, the tobacconist and newsagent with its Swan Vestas advertisement, occupied the site of the original Gotch Bank.

A Section of a county map of northamptonshire showing Kettering and surrounding areas c1850

THE HIGH STREET

THE HIGH STREET 1922 72227

The Royal Hotel (left) vied with the George in attracting a superior local clientele. Next door, the drapers, Pritchard's, has a sun awning to prevent the window display fading. Beyond we can see the façade of the Midland Bank, now HSBC. The neo-Georgian building beyond was to be rebuilt as the Granada Cinema (see K13065, pages 36-37). Lloyds Bank, on the right, is on the corner of Market Street. The policeman, possibly on traffic duty, is talking to a man whose cap and breeches suggest a chauffeur or AA patrolman. Meanwhile a butcher's boy cycles down the middle of the High Street, a reminder that delivery to the door was expected in 1922. Making the deliveries was the first foot on the career rung, followed by serving in the shop.

late 19th century. There had been a silversmith in these shops at the end of Victoria's reign. In 1969 A A Thornton re-opened the premises as a clockmakers and jewellers, re-constructing the interior to look like an old-fashioned shop.

Timpson's shoe shop is next door to the Granada cinema in the High Street (K13065, pages 36-37). William Timpson was one of the rags-to-riches patriarchs of Victorian Kettering. He came from the weaving trade, which was suffering in the middle of the 19th century from advances in machinery that put home workers out of business. William had to work from the age of eight, making leather laces for the Gotch factory. His elder brother Charles had started a shoe shop in Manchester, and in 1860, at the age of eleven, William set off to join him.

In the early railway age there was a great criss-crossing of lines and William got lost in the system, ending up with no money on a platform in Sheffield. The rest of the story is like a Dickens novel. As he stood crying an old gentleman asked him what had happened, and hearing William's story, he took him on the right train and delivered the boy to his brother. Then he vanished before the Timpsons thought of asking his name. After this, young William flourished; he realised that his Lancashire customers had wider-than-average feet, so when he had to return south through ill health, he started a shoe-making workshop in Kettering to make wide fittings for the northern market. He began work in a former silk weaving mill in Market Street (where the Yorkshire Bank is now).

Trade increased until the factory in Market Street, which had always relied largely on outworkers, could not cope with the demand. One of the most modern factories in Britain was built in 1921 in North Park, which was then near the edge of Kettering. An enormous glass structure, it was like a Crystal Palace built beside green playing fields. William Timpson never forgot the old man who had rescued him in 1860. At the firm's annual lunch a toast would be made to 'the unknown benefactor' until William died in 1929.

Timpsons had become gigantic by the 1950s, supplying 22,000 pairs of shoes a week for 262 retail shops. It seemed as if the town would continue its dependence on one trade, but gradually demands for British footwear decreased, and Timpsons sold their great glass factory in 1972.

Pritchard's awning, in the 1922 view of the High Street (72227, above) masks a shop which had long been associated with jewellery. The lower, Georgian, façade of these shops conceals the remains of a 17th-century farmhouse, the yard of which was approached by the archway at the end of Bank Chambers (K13065, pages 36-37) where the architectural offices of Gotch & Saunders were opened in the

THE HIGH STREET

Left: THE HIGH STREET c1960 K13065

This was a junction devoted to money. The Midland Bank is prominent on the left, facing the National Westminster and Barclays, which was a few steps from Lloyds' palatial building opposite the Royal Hotel. By 2000 most of the banks were still in this small area - and still in their opulent buildings. At the right of the Midland Bank is an archway, wide enough for a pony and trap, leading to a cobbled yard and the offices of the town's prestigious architects, Gotch and Saunders. Timpson's Shoes were a chain store with branches all over Britain. The shoes were made just round the corner in Market Street until the 1930s.

Below Left: THE HIGH STREET 1922 72229

Below: THE HIGH STREET c1955 K13027

There is hardly more traffic in 1955 than in 1922; townspeople, however grand, still cycled or walked to work. There was a joke - especially appreciated in a boot and shoe town - that one cycled to save shoe leather. Lloyds Bank had succeeded the Northamptonshire Banking Company, which had opened in 1876 in temporary offices in the Market Place. In 1890 they joined forces with the Capital and Counties Bank.

THE HIGH STREET

THE HIGH STREET c1950 K13023

A smart two-seater convertible is parked outside the imposing Barclays Bank, which had been built in 1910 as the Boston & Spalding Bank. Traffic is still sparse in the town's main shopping street, but parking regulations (different sides on alternate days) were in force. The International Stores, housed in a Georgian building on the left, was in a prime position on the corner of Meadow Road. The store moved from Kettering in 1984 as they could not find suitable, larger premises. Beyond is Charnley & Son, an old-established opticians, which recently closed.

THE HIGH STREET c1955 K13048

The National Westminster Bank (extreme right) is next door to a seed merchant, still an important trader in a country town before seeds were brightly packaged and sold by garden centres. The Countryside Library was next door - genteel libraries charged borrowers. Boots the Chemists' library (behind us, at the corner of Market Street) was upstairs, approached by a wooden staircase. In time their clientele would realise that there was no stigma in borrowing books from a public library, and that the pages were germ-free and not always sticky. Two men's outfitters existed side by side; Dunn & Co were part of a national chain selling 'gentlemanly' clothes: tweed jackets, caps and hats and sturdy gloves which fastened at the wrist with buttons incised with 'Dunns'. The arched Venetian windows of a building of 1880 are still fairly staid, but in 1983 a ritzy V-shaped window would replace the flat front so the customers could see almost all round the display of Foster Bros.

THE HIGH STREET

The Granada (K13065, pages 36-37) had been opened in 1938 as the Regal, but was bought by the Granada chain in the 1950s. This exciting Art Deco building represented luxury to audiences. The auditorium was popularly supposed to seat 1,500, and there was a tea-room on the first floor. The Granada certainly knew how to entertain the public; in the early 1960s they would have a midweek change of programme, and visiting bands and pop stars gave stage shows on Sundays. It was always busy. It is now a bingo hall.

Notice the International Stores with its chamfered corner on the upper floor at the entry to Meadow Road (K13048, left of photograph). This was once Goose Pastures Lane, which led downhill to the gasworks. Almost opposite Meadow Road is Dryland Street, on the right of the High Street. This was once Workhouse Lane, but was re-named after the town doctor who had a surgery here. His neighbour was the local newspaper, the Evening Telegraph, which had offices and printing works close to the town centre for 80 years, but which moved to Northfield Avenue in 1976. After the centre of the High Street began to gravitate around Woolworth's and Marks & Spencer, the site of the Old White Horse would be taken over by Burton's Menswear (K13024, pages 40-41).

The opposite side of the High Street had been re-built in 1862 and was occupied for many years by Webb Brothers. This block and several other buildings in the High Street were the property of the now defunct Grammar School.

The Pavilion cinema (known affectionately as the Pav) was built in 1913 near the place where Boots had their second store by 1960 (K13066, 44-45); although the Gaumont chain took it over, most of its customers still called it by the old, familiar name.

THE HIGH STREET

Only a few steps further along the High Street brings us to some of the multiple stores. Marks & Spencer had replaced F Spence & Son, a furnishers with an impressive window display. Alfred Webb, on the corner of Bellfoundry Lane (left), had been established in 1897 as Webb Bros. By 1950 their façade was discreet, with a cream fascia and neat lettering, but in 1910 it had been vulgarly emblazoned with boards advertising caps, hats and trousers made to measure for 10s 6d. Webbs had branches in ten other towns, so they could safely claim to be 'The Midland Counties Outfitter'. The Old White Horse (right) would become Burton Menswear in 1962. Further down on the left is an upright sign for the Pavilion cinema, which would close in 1959.

THE HIGH STREET c1960 K13081

The first modern shop façade in the High Street was Fine Fare (left), a small supermarket on the corner of Meadow Road, vying with the more old-fashioned International Stores opposite. Its design was typical of an era which produced chrome bumpers and aggressive squared-off car bodies.

BAKEHOUSE HILL (THE HIGH STREET)

This friendly triangle where the High Street and Gold Street meet no longer exists. The area was redeveloped in the 1960s, and now there is a slightly changed layout, with a pedestrianised 'island' with seats and shrubs replacing the old road junction. The original communal town bakehouse stood here in the 16th century. Bell and Billows (K13044, pages 46-47, left) was an ironmongers, built in 1889, and demolished in 1968. The window displays attracted enormous male attention, with large rows of sheath knives and air-rifles. Next door was Theobalds the bakers, which has moved into Lower Street.

Uphill is the old Grammar School (K13044, centre) with a distinctive gabled façade covered with creepers, including a luxuriant wisteria. Most schools are proud to trace their foundation back to Elizabeth I, but Kettering Grammar School was too old for its origins to be recorded. It was probably a relic of the days when there was a chantry school attached to the church. Elizabeth did give aid to the ancient school by endowing it with some Manor House property with rents of £1.24 a year. The school had a chequered history until the 19th century, with eccentric and lazy masters. Finally there were only two or three boys left. The school was re-organised in 1854. A dynamic new master increased

BAKEHOUSE HILL (THE HIGH STREET)

This view looks back towards Woolworth's from Bakehouse Hill, where the mini-roundabout marks the convergence of the High Street, Gold Street and Lower Street. Boots were to move three times, epitomising the changing importance of different parts of the town centre. Here, they have a new building, which had replaced the Pavilion Cinema a year earlier, which they share with Civic and Victor Value, a small supermarket. The late Georgian building next door still has the plaque-like spaces for advertising between the windows on the first and second floors used by Webb Bros in 1910. Halfords, the cycle shop, had to compete with at least three other cycle retailers. They sold bikes on hire purchase at 2/6 a week.

the popularity of the school, and fees were charged according to the parents' means. Two years later there were so many pupils that the 'new' school, which we can see in the photographs, was built in the town centre. It was finished in 1859 in imitation of a Jacobean country house, with a master's lodging on one side. The playground was a lawned garden with two huge chestnuts. In spite of the attractive premises, the school was not a success. The lively master left, and was succeeded by an incompetent one, a Mr Widdowson, who had a handsome salary, along with a continually rising income from ever-increasing rents. As he did nothing to attract new boys, numbers began to dwindle again.

Finally Mr Widdowson accepted a handsome pension and left, but now it was obvious that the school premises were no longer suitable. A new neo-Georgian building was built in Bowling Green Road in 1913. It was large enough to house the Grammar School and a High School for girls. It would have two literary connections: H E Bates, who wrote 'Fair Stood The Wind for France' and the 'Uncle Silas' stories, was a pupil; and for a short time the boys were taught by J L Carr, the well-known novelist.

After the old building was no longer a school it became a doctor's surgery, and then council offices. There is still resentment in Kettering over the way in which it was swiftly demolished in 1964,

BAKEHOUSE HILL (THE HIGH STREET)

in spite of opposition, to make way for a featureless new shopping parade. Other landmarks in picture K13044 (right), which have disappeared are the neighbouring Crown Inn with its white pillared gateway (it had also been part of Ellsworthy's Brewery), and the Odeon, which had been the third cinema in Kettering within a few hundred yards. Altogether there have been six cinemas in the town.

The Odeon (K13044, right) opened in the 1930s. It had the appearance of a radio of the same period, square and boxy with light bands running round its curved corner. It had replaced the older Victoria Hall, which had been a theatre and ballroom since 1888 but which had been turned into a cinema in 1920.

Out of view, on the right, is the Toller Congregational Church. This is heir to the 'Little Meeting' house, and there are traces of a Georgian building, but what Pevsner described as a 'terrible red brick façade with two short towers' now dominates this part of the pedestrianised area.

BAKEHOUSE HILL c1955 K13044

Almost everything in this view has been swept away. Bell & Billows were a remarkable ironmongers in a handsome late Victorian building. The wisteria-covered building on the left going up the hill was the Old Grammar School with the Crown Inn next door. The Odeon was to be demolished in 1974, when shops would be built on the site. In the row of late Georgian shops on the right, two new shop-fronts, Norvic and Sketchley, flank Roberts & Sons, a high-class grocer where loose tea was kept in black and gold canisters and a smell of roasting coffee crept into the outside air. Sketchley were on the site of the first Co-op in the town - it had opened in 1866.

GOLD STREET

The sporty two-seater coupé in photograph 72230 (opposite) has Gold Street pretty much to itself. Motorists rarely met other cars in Kettering town centre, as everywhere was within walking or cycling distance. Frequently, cars belonged to local doctors making home calls. A chemist such as Hitchman's (72230, left of photograph) was often a good substitute for a doctor and did not cost anything. Before the National Health Service came into being, a working class family had to consider if they could afford medical help, although many people were 'on the panel', paying a weekly contribution to a family doctor as insurance for when they were ill.

In another photograph of Gold Street in 1922 (72231, pages 50-51) the high gabled roof and tall chimneys of the Grammar School in the distance make a fitting focal point to the downhill stretch of the Old Post Office Buildings on the right. Designed by Gotch & Saunders, they were faced with distinctive red terracotta and had been built in 1887. The General Post Office was an important feature of the block, which had an arcade forming a passage through to Richard Leys and Tanners Lane behind. All was to be changed in 1974, when the Newborough Centre was erected. There was enormous opposition to the demolition plans. The Kettering Civic Society suggested that the new shopping complex could be built behind the Victorian parade; but it was pulled down, and in its place there is an indoor mall fronted by Boots the Chemist.

By the 1950s, traffic had become one-way in Gold Street, and fluorescent lighting had replaced the wrought-iron lamp standards of 1922 (see K13042, pages 50-51). The Fuller Chapel still remains (72230, right, and K13042, pages 50-51). Palladian architecture appealed to Kettering Victorians; though it was built in 1861, the rounded arches and high pediment of the chapel made it seem much older. The Fuller Chapel would survive when that side of Gold Street had been demolished to build the Newborough shopping centre.

GOLD STREET 1922 72230

Hitchman's, the chemist on the left, was on the corner of Silver Street and Gold Street. Their own medicines were made up in the dispensary, where they made a well-known sulphur pill for skin problems and an 'extract of honey' hand cream. This sort of chemist often had scales for weighing babies, as well as alluring bottles of coloured liquids as window decorations. The young mothers had almost certainly been getting free advice on childcare from Hitchman's. Notice that however poor they were, women wore hats when they went out - even on local errands. This corner would be dominated by Burtons in the 1930s.

GOLD STREET

On the right the Old Post Office Buildings, faced in red terracotta, were a triumphant memorial to the Victorian splendour of the town, and to Gotch and Saunders, the architects.

Studs on the road surface mark the only traffic crossing in Kettering at this date. On the right, Gordon Thoday, with branches throughout East Anglia, sold dress fabrics. Clothes were still made at home, and Thoday sold patterns, often by Vogue, which could cost as much as 7s 6d, and also the more humble and easier designs selling for 1s 9d. By now Hitchman's the chemists had been swept away: Montague Burton had built an art deco emporium (left) on the corner of Silver Street.

SILVER STREET

SILVER STREET c1950 K13018

The only set of traffic lights in
Kettering coped with a trickle of
traffic. Silver Street was a place for
refreshment; the ornate façade of the
Rising Sun is on the right near the
corner of Montagu Street, with a cluster
of cafés like the Hollywood Restaurant
and London Grill. Chalkley's (right),
the drapers, had a handsome shop sign
in large silver letters on a shiny black
background. At one point there were
ten Chalkley shops in the area until
the call-up in the Second World War
resulted in a loss of staff - and they
dwindled to this one shop.

SILVER STREET c1955 K13022

This view down Silver Street, widened here at the junction with Gold Street in the 1930s, looks towards Dalkieth Place. The 'new look' in
fashions is demonstrated by the young woman crossing the street with her more dowdy companion; longer skirts, wider shoulders and a
nipped-in waist were signs of relaxation from wartime clothing restrictions. Burton's Menswear, on the right of the photograph, sold suits off
the peg or made to measure - all on easy payments.

SILVER STREET

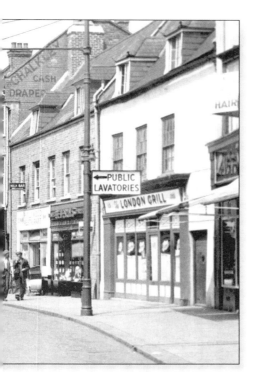

Road widening in 1933 had resulted in the demolition of one side of the street. Before, the most imposing building had been a Wesleyan chapel; when this was taken down, the new eyecatcher was the white 1930s block built for Burton's (K13022, page 52, on the right of the photograph, and K13064, below), which would become Eastern Carpet Stores by 1960. Any kind of men's tailoring had short shrift in Kettering between the two world wars, when the Kaycee factory flourished in nearby Field Street. When Montague Burton, 'The Tailor of Taste,' opened his art deco premises, Kaycee (derived from Kettering Co-operative) had three factories in the town employing 2,000 workers. Co-op suits were made to measure for £2 7s 6d.

As the High Street became pedestrianised, the surrounding streets like Silver Street and Montagu Street became commercially less popular. The Eastern Carpet Stores replaced the 'Tailor of Taste', and a shoe repair shop and Robinson Rentals (radio and TV) took over the Gold Street frontage.

The Rising Sun public house near the corner of Montagu Street (K13022), decorated with oriel windows and plaster swags, is a monument to Victorian prosperity. Campbells, 'the universal furnishers' (K13018, opposite, on the left), were on the corner of Ebenezer Place, a little lane running back into Gold Street. It is still there, proving that some of the eccentricity of the old town has survived.

SILVER STREET c1960 K13064

Burton's can be seen in the middle of this photograph, the white building by the white van and delivery lorry,

SILVER STREET

SILVER STREET c1960 K13062

As neo-Georgian buildings replaced the older local shops, the shopping centre of Kettering also developed wth nation-wide multiple stores. Jax, a cheerful low-price dress shop for younger customers, replaced the more staid Co-op; Millett's, which began by selling army surplus goods, branched into camping equipment and tough outdoor clothes. Chalkley's Victorian upper façade was replaced by a flat frontage (K13064, page 53).

KETTERING FROM THE AIR 1937 AF53709

Newland Street

The Co-op still had scattered shops along the street, alongside Lillian Worrall (dresses for smart ladies) and H Winstone (tobaccos) with their elaborate Abdullah sign for Turkish cigarettes. On the opposite side is the Fleur-de-Lys public house, popularly called the Flue, which once had a license to serve early morning alcohol to furnace workers coming off the night shift.

NEWLAND STREET

The Co-operative movement was very vigorous in Kettering, and Newland Street became its showpiece. The first shop in town even pre-dated the famous Rochdale co-op pioneers of 1848. It was established in 1829, when the town was going through hard times with little employment in the weaving trade, and before the manufacture of boots and shoes had become the main industry; Kettering had 3,000 inhabitants, living in primitive cottages. The shop failed, probably because it was underfunded. In 1866 the Co-op started again with 60 members, only two of whom could afford to pay the £1 share; the others invested at 4d a week. The 'shop' was a front room of a house in the High Street, and a committee member walked to Northampton and back to buy the first orders. They survived, and opened their first real shop in 1868. They expanded to two shops, and set up their own bakery. Kettering Co-operative gathered momentum. It soon had an educational section, its own magazine, a choral society and flower shows; there were even scholarships to help keep bright children at school. Kettering Co-op (KICS) ended with seventeen stores all over the town and in nearby villages. Increasingly self-sufficient, the Co-op even became landlords at the end of the 19th century, when they built 100 houses on the northern reaches of Kettering

Such an influential organisation had to have important premises. A magnificent drapery store was opened in Newland Street in 1893, with oriel windows echoing those of the Rising Sun in nearby Silver Street. An arcade and central store were opened linking Newland and Montagu Streets (we can see the Central Arcade entrance porch to the right in K13019 opposite). The building included a large meeting hall. The Labour government was in power at the time, and on the day of the opening ceremony the Prime Minister, Ramsay Macdonald, sent a jocular message to KICS, asking them not to deprive him of his whole cabinet, for three government ministers attended. As supermarkets and multiple stores opened in Kettering, the Co-op became less important, although outlying stores in large villages remained. A KICS supermarket was finally opened in the 'new' area of Northfield Avenue, which replaced all the various stores of the past. The Kaycee clothing factory shut in 1975, and by 1978 KICS had to amalgamate with Leicestershire Co-op.

Newland Street was not entirely owned by the KICS. Next door to Woodcock's corner store was the Mikado café, comfortably situated for Kettering ladies to have tea while they shopped (see K13019). It belonged to the baker's, Barlow's, who had several other cafes in the town. It was renovated in the 1930s to look like a Georgian house, with a first floor bowed window in which customers could take tea and watch the traffic at the crossroads. The ground floor shop window had displays of elaborate wedding cakes.

NEWLAND STREET 1922 72235

This junction of Newland Street with Gold Street, Silver Street and Montagu Street was sometimes busy enough to have policemen on point duty. By the post-war period traffic had increased, so traffic lights were installed (see K13018, pages 52). The KICS (Co-op) drapery building with Jacobean bay windows can be seen down Newland Street. Ernest Woodcock, on the right, extended down Montagu Street and was described as Kettering's leading department store for fashions, fabrics, furnishings, furniture and household linen. They were also funeral directors.

MONTAGU STREET

MONTAGU STREET c1950 K13021

Stamford Road School can be seen in the distance. Built in 1892, it was the first Kettering school to be built under the national system for non-denominational education, but it managed to appear ecclesiastical with its imposing clock tower. Near the camera, and close to the traffic lights, we see Paul Taylor (radio and TV) and George Bird (fruit and veg). Mr Bird, who also had a stall on the market, went to Covent Garden twice a week to buy produce that would arrive by train in Kettering by lunchtime.

Montagu Street

This street, with its idiosyncratic spelling, commemorates the surname of the Dukes of Buccleuch. Originally Scottish landowners, the Scott-Montagu family was to increase in importance when a daughter married the Duke of Monmouth, who was the illegitimate son of Charles II, and who would later lead the Monmouth rebellion in 1685. The Buccleuchs' Northamptonshire estate is close to Kettering, and parts of the town are named after family titles: Dalkeith Place and Buccleuch Street. The Conservative Club, half way along Montagu Street (K13041, opposite), was built on land donated by the duke.

The Robinson car was made for Robinson's garage, which opened here in 1905. Only three were constructed; BD983, in the Manor House museum, was first registered on 1 April 1910, but it was built in 1907 in an engineering works in nearby Victoria Street, which belonged to the grandfather of the garage owner, Charles Robinson. It was 12-horsepower (1884cc), and had a unique cooling system in which the exhaust gases were used to propel fresh air round the engine.

Ernest Woodcock's department store was on the corner of Montagu and Newland Streets (K13021, pages 62-63). It was built in 1899 and was very citified for a small provincial town, with several floors selling gowns and millinery and with a brass overhead rail system for returning change to counters from a central cashier's office. It was later taken over by the Co-op. Half way down Montagu Street there was an alternative entrance to the Co-op arcade and central meeting hall.

Montagu Street c1955 K13041

At the Stamford Road end of the street, the newly-built showroom of Tutty's sold kitchen units and appliances. Newman's next door was an old-fashioned ironmongers, which has resisted change. Further down, past a wool shop, is the large brick-built Kettering Conservative Club, built on a site donated by the Duke of Buccleuch in 1876. It opened in 1889, the same year as the Liberal Club in Dalkeith Place.

The Schools and the Council Offices

Above: THE GRAMMAR SCHOOL AND THE HIGH SCHOOL 1922 72243

This palatial neo-Georgian building was opened in 1913 as the boys' Grammar School, in the right part of the building, and the girls' High School on the left. The central block held art rooms and other communal areas, but great effort was made to keep the sexes separate. In the early 1960s the Grammar School moved to a new building in Windmill Avenue, and the Borough Council took over the building.

Below: THE GRAMMAR SCHOOL c1960 K13074

The newly-opened Grammar School at the end of Windmill Avenue. A ceramic mural on the front by William Mitchell demonstrated the progressiveness of the architects. The school was to close, and the building then became the Art Department of the Tresham Institute.

NORTHFIELD AVENUE

Curving in a crescent from Northampton Road to Rockingham Road, the avenue started as a residential development at its northern end, where it is close to the football ground of the 'Poppies' on Rockingham Road.

As businesses moved out of the town centre, Northfield Avenue became an attractive commercial site. The cattle market moved here in 1967. (It would close altogether in 1992.) It would be followed by the local newspaper - the Evening Telegraph, or the E T - in 1976. Soon DIY stores followed, with petrol stations and car showrooms. Finally, in the 1980s, the Co-op superstore was built close to the residential section of the avenue.

Above: NORTHFIELD GARDENS c1960 K13055

Below: NORTHFIELD AVENUE c1955 K13054

THE PLEASURE PARK, ROCKINGHAM ROAD

Charles Wicksteed founded an engineering works in Kettering in 1876. He had started work in Leeds, where he designed steam ploughs. Beginning with the manufacture of machine tools, he went on to design a motor gearbox in 1907, but in 1914 his factory made munitions. He believed in the nationalisation of land, and when he became a town councillor, he persuaded the council to buy land in the growing residential area off Rockingham Road. It provided a play area for children from the terraced streets round the factories, as well as from those avenues built by the Co-op to the north. It is enjoyed by adults too, especially the elderly.

The bandstand, built in the 1930s, had a regular programme of music (K13058, opposite). Sometimes there were concerts by the famous brass band of Munn & Felton. This band had been started by Frederick Felton, a partner in a boot factory. He was another self-made man; he started his career selling bootlaces door-to-door. He had also been a bandsman in the Salvation Army, so he was experienced when he set up his works' band. It was to win prizes throughout the world.

ROCKINGHAM ROAD PLEASURE PARK,
THE BANDSTAND c1955 K13058

THE PLEASURE PARK, ROCKINGHAM ROAD

Above: ROCKINGHAM ROAD PLEASURE PARK
c1960 K13057

Brass bands played regularly in the bandstand, which was erected in the early 1930s. The chained-off area was reserved for the paying audience, who could hire folding chairs; but free concerts could be enjoyed by anybody who sat on the grass outside the inner circle. The path through the park was supposed to follow the route of a Roman road.

Top Right: THE BOWLING GREEN,
ROCKINGHAM PLEASURE PARK c1965 K13113

Once there had been a bowling green near the town centre, commemorated by Bowling Green Road. When Charles Wicksteed opened the park, bowls and putting became popular with the people who lived nearby.

Bottom Right: THE PUTTING GREEN c1960 K13059

THE PLEASURE PARK, ROCKINGHAM ROAD

AN ORDNANCE SURVEY MAP SHOWING KETTERING AND SURROUNDING AREAS 1885

Wicksteed Park

The Bridge, Wicksteed Park c1955 K13003

WICKSTEED PARK

After the First World War, Charles Wicksteed diverted from munitions into playground equipment. It was a time when enlightened councils were setting up public parks and recreation grounds with swings and slides. He shared his success with Kettering by buying 150 acres on the edge of the town on the way to the village of Barton Seagrave. He had turned it into an enormous playground for children by 1921; it had two boating lakes, and a model railway with two locomotives called King Arthur and The Lady of the Lake (K13051, pages 84-85).

Coaches brought visitors from all over the East Midlands. Use of the simpler equipment was always meant to be free, but as the attractions became more complicated a ticket system was brought in. A famous professional cycle track was built in the park in the late 1950s.

THE PARK GATES c1965 K13091
The park gates were on Pytchley Road.

WICKSTEED PARK

THE BOATING LAKE c1965 K13107

The Boating Lake c1955 K13016

The boating lake covered 30 acres. The smaller lake, for younger children, was separated from the larger one by a hump-backed bridge (K13007, pages 76-77).

WICKSTEED PARK, THE CHILDREN'S PLAYGROUND c1955 K13008
Even a simple sandpit was a novelty in an age before sandpits were common in back gardens.

WICKSTEED PARK

WICKSTEED PARK

Left: WICKSTEED PARK c1955 K13011

The 'jungle' bridges were to divert youngsters away from the formal flower gardens - and to give the adults a rest.

Below: WICKSTEED PARK c1960 K13039

The lakeside railway makes a circuit of the boating lake and the paddling pool. Most of the park was devoted to children's amusements, but there was one backwater for swans.

WICKSTEED PARK

Left: WICKSTEED PARK,
THE RAILWAY c1960 K13051

Below: WICKSTEED PARK,
THE PAVILION c1955 K13005

The pavilion in the park became popular locally for celebrations and company dinners. One of Charles Wicksteed's inventions was a machine for the tearooms, which cut and buttered bread. As he grew older, Charles Wicksteed would often visit the park in a two-seater car, with his terrier, Jerry, sitting in the passenger seat. In 1927 Jerry disappeared on one of these outings. He was never found, and in his memory his master had a statue erected in the gardens of the park, with a commemorative verse:

'Closely bound to a human heart,
Little brown dog, you had your part
In the levelling, building, staying of streams
In the Park that arose from your Master's dreams.'

NAMES OF SUBSCRIBERS

FRANCIS FRITH'S
TOWN&CITY
MEMORIES

The following people have kindly supported this book by purchasing limited edition copies prior to publication.

In memory of Mr and Mrs F R Allsopp of Kettering

In memory of Jessie Bradshaw

The Beal Family, Kettering 2005

Mervyn G Bellamy

The Bishop Family, Kettering

Kenneth Blackwell, Kettering, Northants

John Carter

The Collins Family, Kettering

Liz Cooke, Kettering

Luke Cotter - In memory of mum and dad

John T Cowan, Kettering

Wendy and Richard Curtis

In memory of Henry Walter Taffs Dawson

Mr W K Dobson

Nick Elliott, Kettering

The Evans Family, Kettering

Trevor Flude, Kettering

Mrs Susan Gale, Mr Michael Gale

John Garlick and Family, Kettering

Mr G Goodey and Mrs S M Goodey, Kettering

Veronica, née Harley, daughter of Les and Con

For my dad, Michael Harris

Mr H P and Mrs B M Hodges

Philip Hollobone

The Horden Family, Kettering

Mr and Mrs W H Hulme, Kettering

In memory of my Mother, Lilian M Jervis

Peter, Thomas and Joseph Jones

To my wonderful husband, Richard, love Judith

William and Kay Leigh, Rebecca and Keiran

Gordon Robert Langley

Brian Paling

Janet Paling

John and Ruby Pearson, Kettering, July 2006

Tony and Sue Pulford's Family, Kettering

Mr Alan and Mrs Alison Reed and Family

Mr G F K and Mrs S Rogers, Kettering

Mr E and Mrs J W Rylott

Kevin W Sawford, Kettering

www.ketteringweb.com by Paul Sugden

Bronwen Viggars 24/07/46

To Rex Walpole, love Melvin and Family

To John Walton on his 60th Birthday

Toney and Elaine Warren, Woodford

Christine Weston 14/03/53

Mr and Mrs F C York, Kettering

INDEX

FURTHER READING

A Kettering Kaleidoscope by Ian Addis and Barrie Chambers. Diametric Publications 1999, £9.95.
Personal views of life in Kettering by two boys growing up in the 1950s.

Kettering Revisited. Kettering Civic Society 1984.

Old Kettering - A View from the 1930s, Volumes 1-4 Tony Ireson. Published by the author 1988 to 1994, £5.95.
These entrancing paperbacks are filled with entertaining reminiscences.

Kettering Then and Now by Ian Addis and Robert Mercer. Jemma Publications 1988, £7.99.

Kettering Revisited, Pictures from the Past by Tony Smith. W D Wharton 1999, £14.99.

Northamptonshire by Nikolaus Pevsner, 'Buildings of England' series. Penguin 1961 onwards.

The above publications have been used extensively in writing this book.

The Francis Frith Collection Titles

www.francisfrith.co.uk

The Francis Frith Collection publishes over 100 new titles each year. A selection of those currently available is listed below. For latest catalogue please contact The Francis Frith Collection. **Town Books** 96 pages, approximately 75 photos. **County and Themed Books** 128 pages, approximately 135 photos (unless specified).

Accrington Old and New
Alderley Edge and Wilmslow
Amersham, Chesham and Rickmansworth
Andover
Around Abergavenny
Around Alton
Aylesbury
Barnstaple
Bedford
Bedfordshire
Berkshire Living Memories
Berkshire Pocket Album
Blackpool Pocket Album
Bognor Regis
Bournemouth
Bradford
Bridgend
Bridport
Brighton and Hove
Bristol
Buckinghamshire
Calne Living Memories
Camberley Pocket Album
Canterbury Cathedral
Cardiff Old and New
Chatham and the Medway Towns
Chelmsford
Chepstow Then and Now
Cheshire
Cheshire Living Memories
Chester
Chesterfield
Chigwell
Christchurch
Churches of East Cornwall
Clevedon
Clitheroe
Corby Living Memories
Cornish Coast
Cornwall Living Memories
Cotswold Living Memories
Cotswold Pocket Album
Coulsdon, Chipstead and Woodmanstern
County Durham
Cromer, Sheringham and Holt
Dartmoor Pocket Album
Derby
Derbyshire
Derbyshire Living Memories
Devon
Devon Churches
Dorchester

Dorset Coast Pocket Album
Dorset Living Memories
Dorset Villages
Down the Dart
Down the Severn
Down the Thames
Dunmow, Thaxted and Finchingfield
Durham
East Anglia Pocket Album
East Devon
East Grinstead
Edinburgh
Ely and The Fens
Essex Pocket Album
Essex Second Selection
Essex: The London Boroughs
Exeter
Exmoor
Falmouth
Farnborough, Fleet and Aldershot
Folkestone
Frome
Furness and Cartmel Peninsulas
Glamorgan
Glasgow
Glastonbury
Gloucester
Gloucestershire
Greater Manchester
Guildford
Hailsham
Hampshire
Harrogate
Hastings and Bexhill
Haywards Heath Living Memories
Heads of the Valleys
Heart of Lancashire Pocket Album
Helston
Herefordshire
Horsham
Humberside Pocket Album
Huntingdon, St Neots and St Ives
Hythe, Romney Marsh and Ashford
Ilfracombe
Ipswich Pocket Album
Isle of Wight
Isle of Wight Living Memories
King's Lynn
Kingston upon Thames
Lake District Pocket Album
Lancashire Living Memories
Lancashire Villages

Available from your local bookshop or from the publisher

The Francis Frith Collection Titles (continued)

Lancaster, Morecambe and Heysham Pocket Album
Leeds Pocket Album
Leicester
Leicestershire
Lincolnshire Living Memoires
Lincolnshire Pocket Album
Liverpool and Merseyside
London Pocket Album
Ludlow
Maidenhead
Maidstone
Malmesbury
Manchester Pocket Album
Marlborough
Matlock
Merseyside Living Memories
Nantwich and Crewe
New Forest
Newbury Living Memories
Newquay to St Ives
North Devon Living Memories
North London
North Wales
North Yorkshire
Northamptonshire
Northumberland
Northwich
Nottingham
Nottinghamshire Pocket Album
Oakham
Odiham Then and Now
Oxford Pocket Album
Oxfordshire
Padstow
Pembrokeshire
Penzance
Petersfield Then and Now
Plymouth
Poole and Sandbanks
Preston Pocket Album
Ramsgate Old and New
Reading Pocket Album
Redditch Living Memories
Redhill to Reigate
Richmond
Ringwood
Rochdale
Romford Pocket Album
Salisbury Pocket Album
Scotland
Scottish Castles
Sevenoaks and Tonbridge
Sheffield and South Yorkshire Pocket Album
Shropshire
Somerset
South Devon Coast
South Devon Living Memories
South East London
Southampton Pocket Album
Southend Pocket Album
Southport

Southwold to Aldeburgh
Stourbridge Living Memories
Stratford upon Avon
Stroud
Suffolk
Suffolk Pocket Album
Surrey Living Memories
Sussex
Sutton
Swanage and Purbeck
Swansea Pocket Album
Swindon Living Memories
Taunton
Teignmouth
Tenby and Saundersfoot
Tiverton
Torbay
Truro
Uppingham
Villages of Kent
Villages of Surrey
Villages of Sussex Pocket Album
Wakefield and the Five Towns Living Memories
Warrington
Warwick
Warwickshire Pocket Album
Wellingborough Living Memories
Wells
Welsh Castles
West Midlands Pocket Album
West Wiltshire Towns
West Yorkshire
Weston-super-Mare
Weymouth
Widnes and Runcorn
Wiltshire Churches
Wiltshire Living Memories
Wiltshire Pocket Album
Wimborne
Winchester Pocket Album
Windermere
Windsor
Wirral
Wokingham and Bracknell
Woodbridge
Worcester
Worcestershire
Worcestershire Living Memories
Wyre Forest
York Pocket Album
Yorkshire
Yorkshire Coastal Memories
Yorkshire Dales
Yorkshire Revisited

See Frith books on the internet at www.francisfrith.co.uk

FRITH PRODUCTS & SERVICES

Francis Frith would doubtless be pleased to know that the pioneering publishing venture he started in 1860 still continues today. Over a hundred and forty years later, The Francis Frith Collection continues in the same innovative tradition and is now one of the foremost publishers of vintage photographs in the world. Some of the current activities include:

Interior Decoration

Today Frith's photographs can be seen framed and as giant wall murals in thousands of pubs, restaurants, hotels, banks, retail stores and other public buildings throughout the country. In every case they enhance the unique local atmosphere of the places they depict and provide reminders of gentler days in an increasingly busy and frenetic world.

Product Promotions

Frith products are used by many major companies to promote the sales of their own products or to reinforce their own history and heritage. Frith promotions have been used by Hovis bread, Courage beers, Scots Porage Oats, Colman's mustard, Cadbury's foods, Mellow Birds coffee, Dunhill pipe tobacco, Guinness, and Bulmer's Cider.

Genealogy and Family History

As the interest in family history and roots grows world-wide, more and more people are turning to Frith's photographs of Great Britain for images of the towns, villages and streets where their ancestors lived; and, of course, photographs of the churches and chapels where their ancestors were christened, married and buried are an essential part of every genealogy tree and family album.

Frith Products

All Frith photographs are available Framed or just as Mounted Prints and Posters (size 23 x 16 inches). These may be ordered from the address below. From time to time other products - Address Books, Calendars, Table Mats, etc - are available.

The Internet

Already ninety thousand Frith photographs can be viewed and purchased on the internet through the Frith websites and a myriad of partner sites.

For more detailed information on Frith companies and products, look at these sites:

www.francisfrith.co.uk
www.francisfrith.com
(for North American visitors)

See the complete list of Frith Books at:

www.francisfrith.co.uk

This web site is regularly updated with the latest list of publications from The Francis Frith Collection. If you wish to buy books relating to another part of the country that your local bookshop does not stock, you may purchase on-line.

For further information, trade, or author enquiries please contact us at the address below:
The Francis Frith Collection, Frith's Barn, Teffont, Salisbury, Wiltshire, England SP3 5QP.
Tel: +44 (0)1722 716 376 Fax: +44 (0)1722 716 881 Email: sales@francisfrith.co.uk

See Frith books on the internet at www.francisfrith.co.uk

FREE PRINT OF YOUR CHOICE

Mounted Print
Overall size 14 x 11 inches (355 x 280mm)

Choose any Frith photograph in this book.
Simply complete the Voucher opposite and return it with your remittance for £2.25 (to cover postage and handling) and we will print the photograph of your choice in SEPIA (size 11 x 8 inches) and supply it in a cream mount with a burgundy rule line (overall size 14 x 11 inches).
Please note: photographs with a reference number starting with a "Z" are not Frith photographs and cannot be supplied under this offer.
Offer valid for delivery to one UK address only.

PLUS: **Order additional Mounted Prints at HALF PRICE - £7.49 each** (normally £14.99)
If you would like to order more Frith prints from this book, possibly as gifts for friends and family, you can buy them at half price (with no additional postage and handling costs).

PLUS: **Have your Mounted Prints framed**
For an extra £14.95 per print you can have your mounted print(s) framed in an elegant polished wood and gilt moulding, overall size 16 x 13 inches (no additional postage and handling required).

IMPORTANT!

These special prices are only available if you use this form to order. You must use the ORIGINAL VOUCHER on this page (no copies permitted). We can only despatch to one UK address. This offer cannot be combined with any other offer.

Send completed Voucher form to:
The Francis Frith Collection, Frith's Barn, Teffont, Salisbury, Wiltshire SP3 5QP

CHOOSE A PHOTOGRAPH FROM THIS BOOK

 *for **FREE** and Reduced Price Frith Prints*

Please do not photocopy this voucher. Only the original is valid, so please fill it in, cut it out and return it to us with your order.

Picture ref no	Page no	Qty	Mounted @ £7.49	Framed + £14.95	Total Cost £
		1	Free of charge*	£	£
			£7.49	£	£
			£7.49	£	£
			£7.49	£	£
			£7.49	£	£
			£7.49	£	£

Please allow 28 days for delivery. Offer available to one UK address only

* Post & handling	£2.25
Total Order Cost	£

Title of this book . . . .

I enclose a cheque/postal order for £ . . . . made payable to 'The Francis Frith Collection'

OR please debit my Mastercard / Visa / Maestro card, details below

Card Number

Issue No (Maestro only)   Valid from (Maestro)

Expires   Signature

Name Mr/Mrs/Ms . . . .

Address . . . .

. . . .

. . . .

. . . . Postcode . . . .

Daytime Tel No . . . .

Email . . . .

ISBN 1-84589-038-8   Valid to 31/12/08

Free Print – see overleaf

Can you help us with information about any of the Frith photographs in this book?

We are gradually compiling an historical record for each of the photographs in the Frith archive. It is always fascinating to find out the names of the people shown in the pictures, as well as insights into the shops, buildings and other features depicted.

If you recognize anyone in the photographs in this book, or if you have information not already included in the author's caption, do let us know. We would love to hear from you, and will try to publish it in future books or articles.

Our production team

Frith books are produced by a small dedicated team at offices in the converted Grade II listed 18th-century barn at Teffont near Salisbury, illustrated above. Most have worked with the Frith Collection for many years. All have in common one quality: they have a passion for the Frith Collection. The team is constantly expanding, but currently includes:

Paul Baron, Jason Buck, John Buck, Heather Crisp, David Davies, Louis du Mont, Isobel Hall, Lucy Hart, Julian Hight, Peter Horne, James Kinnear, Karen Kinnear, Tina Leary, Stuart Login, Sue Molloy, Sarah Roberts, Kate Rotondetto, Dean Scource, Eliza Sackett, Terence Sackett, Sandra Sampson, Adrian Sanders, Sandra Sanger, Julia Skinner, Miles Smith, Lewis Taylor, Shelley Tolcher, Lorraine Tuck, Miranda Tunnicliffe, David Turner and Ricky Williams.

OCR GCSE MATHEMATICS
STAGES

3

4

GRADUATED
ASSESSMENT

R

SECOND EDITION

- Howard Baxter
- Michael Handbury
- John Jeskins
- Jean Matthews
- Mark Patmore

Hodder Murray
www.hoddereducation.co.uk

Hodder Headline's policy is to use papers that are natural, renewable and recyclable products and made from wood grown in sustainable forests. The logging and manufacturing processes are expected to conform to the environmental regulations of the country of origin.

Orders: please contact Bookpoint Ltd, 130 Milton Park, Abingdon, Oxon OX14 4SB. Telephone: (44) 01235 827720. Fax: (44) 01235 400454. Lines are open 9 a.m. to 5 p.m., Monday to Saturday, with a 24-hour message-answering service. Visit our website at www.hoddereducation.co.uk.

Personal Tutor CD-ROM © Howard Baxter, Michael Handbury, John Jeskins, Jean Matthews, Mark Patmore, Brian Seager, Eddie Wilde, 2007; with contributions from Andy Sturman; developed by Infuze Limited; cast: Nicolette Landau; recorded at Alchemy Soho

First published in 2007 by
Hodder Murray, an imprint of Hodder Education,
a member of the Hodder Headline Group
338 Euston Road
London NW1 3BH

Impression number   10 9 8 7 6 5 4 3 2 1
Year   2012 2011 2010 2009 2008 2007

Cover photo © Andy Sacks/Photographer's Choice/Getty Images
Typeset in 12pt Futura by Tech-Set Ltd. Gateshead, Tyne and Wear.
Printed in Great Britain by CPI Bath

A catalogue record for this title is available from the British Library

ISBN: 978 0340 915 875

Stage 3 Contents

STAG

3

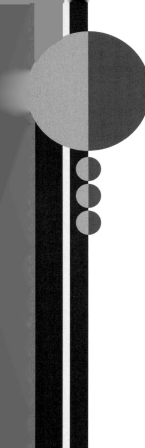

Introduction

This book contains exercises designed to be used with the Graduated Assessment for OCR GCSE Mathematics course. The work covers Stages 3 and 4 of the specification.

Each exercise matches an exercise in the Graduated Assessment for OCR GCSE Mathematics Stages 3 and 4 Student's Book. The exercises in the textbook are numbered through each chapter. For instance, in Chapter 16 in Stage 4, Exercise 16.2 is on using flow charts to solve problems. The corresponding homework exercise is Exercise 16.2H.

You will find that the homework exercises are generally shorter than those in the Student's Book but still cover the same mathematics. Some questions are intended to be completed without a calculator, just as in the Student's Book. These are shown with a non-calculator icon in the same way. Doing these questions without a calculator is vital practice for the non-calculator sections of the module tests and the GCSE examination papers.

The Homework Book gives you the opportunity for further practice on the work undertaken in class. It is also a smaller book to carry home! If you have understood the topics, you should be able to tackle these exercises confidently as they are no harder than the ones you have done in class.

More practice helps to reinforce the ideas you have learned and makes them easier to remember at a later stage. If, however, you do forget, further help is at hand. As well as the textbook, there is also, with this book, a Personal Tutor CD-ROM. This contains worked examples on key topics to revise concepts you find difficult and consolidate your understanding. The exercises supported with examples on the Personal Tutor CD-ROM are marked with an icon.

You will find the answers to this Homework Book in the Foundation Assessment Pack.

Multiplying and dividing

In questions **1** to **20**, find the answer to the calculation.

1 0.7×5	**11** 8.4×5
2 0.3×9	**12** 8.3×6
3 0.6×8	**13** 9.7×2
4 1.8×4	**14** 13.6×8
5 3.6×7	**15** 18.7×6
6 1.6×5	**16** 13.4×4
7 4.3×9	**17** 15.9×8
8 5.6×8	**18** 24.8×5
9 7.8×4	**19** 36.9×8
10 8.6×3	**20** 42.1×7

In questions **21** and **22**, solve the problem.

21 A paving slab is 59·5 cm long.
What is the length of a path made by laying nine of these slabs in a line?

22 A carriage in a train is 29·8 m long.
What is the total length of four carriages?

STAG
3

EXERCISE 1.2H

In questions **1** to **20**, find the answer to the calculation.

1 $0.8 \div 4$ **11** $37.6 \div 8$

2 $2.4 \div 8$ **12** $32.9 \div 7$

3 $7.2 \div 3$ **13** $28.2 \div 3$

4 $8.5 \div 5$ **14** $48.5 \div 5$

5 $7.5 \div 3$ **15** $37.5 \div 3$

6 $1.8 \div 6$ **16** $54.0 \div 4$

7 $3.6 \div 9$ **17** $32.4 \div 6$

8 $4.2 \div 7$ **18** $57.6 \div 3$

9 $8.1 \div 9$ **19** $41.3 \div 7$

10 $2.8 \div 7$ **20** $76.0 \div 8$

In questions **21** and **22**, solve the problem.

21 A stack of 12 textbooks is 22.2 cm high. What is the height of a single textbook?

22 A packet of six large dice weighs 83.4 g. What is the weight of one dice?

EXERCISE 1.3H

1 Multiply each of these numbers by 10.

  a) 37 **b)** 78 **c)** 0.7 **d)** 0.5 **e)** 0.03

2 Multiply each of these numbers by 100.

  a) 37 **b)** 78 **c)** 0.7 **d)** 0.5 **e)** 0.03

3 Multiply each of these numbers by 1000.

  a) 37   **b)** 78   **c)** 0·7   **d)** 0·5   **e)** 0·03

4 Divide each of these numbers by 10.

  a) 73   **b)** 21   **c)** 67   **d)** 29·7   **e)** 5·26

5 Divide each of these numbers by 100.

  a) 73   **b)** 21   **c)** 67   **d)** 29·7   **e)** 5·26

6 Divide each of these numbers by 1000.

  a) 73   **b)** 21   **c)** 67   **d)** 29·7   **e)** 5·26

7 Work out these.

  a) 3·6 × 1 000 000   **b)** 18·7 × 10 000

  c) 821 ÷ 10 000   **d)** 375·1 ÷ 100 000

8 On a model of a building, all distances are multiplied by 100 to find the distance on the real building.
The height of the model is 12 cm.
What is the height of the real building?

9 On a road map, all real distances are divided by 100 000 to get the distance on the map.
What is the distance between two towns on the map that are 27 km apart in reality?

10 A microscope enlarges objects so that they appear to be 1000 times their real length.
An object is really 0·07 mm across.
How far across will it appear to be under the microscope?

STA

2 Time

EXERCISE 2.1H

1 Write these times on the 24-hour clock.

a) 4:20 p.m.   **b)** 5:55 a.m.

c) 11:15 p.m.   **d)** 7:42 a.m.

e) 12:45 p.m.   **f)** 10:35 a.m.

g) 1:25 p.m.   **h)** 1:55 a.m.

2 Write these times on the 12-hour clock.

a) 0500   **b)** 1220

c) 2340   **d)** 0150

e) 2000   **f)** 1707

g) 0225   **h)** 0040

i) 1053   **j)** 1945

3 How long is there between 1635 and midnight?

4 A train left Plymouth at 2:20 p.m. and arrived at Bristol $1\frac{3}{4}$ hours later.
What time did the train arrive in Bristol?

5 A train left Wakefield at 11:20 a.m. and arrived in London at 1:15 p.m.
How long did the journey take?

6 A television news programme lasted for 35 minutes.
It finished at 7:05 p.m.
At what time did the programme start?

7 A flight from London to Washington took $7\frac{1}{2}$ hours.
The flight left London at 1050.
What was the time in London when the flight landed in Washington?

8 The train from Birmingham to Stansted Airport was 57 minutes late.
It arrived at 1843.
At what time should it have arrived?

STA

Squares and square roots

EXERCISE 3.1H

Do not use your calculator for questions **1** to **4**.

1 Write down the square of each of these numbers.

a) 3 **b)** 4 **c)** 7 **d)** 9 **e)** 12

2 Write down the positive square root of each of these numbers.

a) 4 **b)** 25 **c)** 36 **d)** 64 **e)** 121

3 Work out these.

a) 6^2 **b)** 1^2 **c)** 10^2 **d)** 5^2 **e)** 11^2

4 Work out these.

a) $\sqrt{49}$ **b)** $\sqrt{9}$ **c)** $\sqrt{81}$

d) $\sqrt{100}$ **e)** $\sqrt{1}$

You may use your calculator for question **5**.

5 Work out these.

a) $\sqrt{1156}$ **b)** $\sqrt{961}$ **c)** $\sqrt{1764}$

d) $\sqrt{3600}$ **e)** $\sqrt{5625}$ **f)** 17^2

g) 14^2 **h)** 18^2 **i)** 100^2

j) 38^2

Work out these.

1 $8^2 - 6^2$

2 $4^2 + 5^2$

3 $7^2 - 3^2$

4 $6^2 - 3^2$

5 $7^2 + 4^2$

6 $5^2 - 2^2$

7 $5^2 + 6^2 + 7^2$

8 $15^2 - 8^2 - 7^2$

9 $22^2 - 15^2 + 7^2$

10 $15^2 + 16^2 - 17^2$

STA

4 Formulae

EXERCISE 4.1H

1 The total number of seats in an assembly hall is found by multiplying the number of rows by 20.
How many seats are there when there are
  a) 20 rows?   **b)** 15 rows?
  c) 17 rows?   **d)** 13 rows?

2 The perimeter of a square is found by multiplying the length of one side by 4.
Work out the perimeter of a square with sides of these lengths.
  a) 5 cm   **b)** 13 cm
  c) $6\frac{1}{2}$ cm   **d)** 8·2 cm

3 The cost of a child's bus fare is half the cost of an adult's fare.
What is the cost of a child's fare when the adult fare is
  a) 80p?   **b)** 70p?
  c) £1·30?   **d)** £2·36?

4 Five friends divide a bag of sweets equally. To work out how many sweets each person receives, divide the total number of sweets by 5.
How many sweets does each person receive when the bag contains
  a) 20 sweets?   **b)** 55 sweets?
  c) 80 sweets?   **d)** 125 sweets?

5 The time, in minutes, needed to cook a piece of beef can be found by multiplying the weight of the beef in kilograms by 40.
How long does it take to cook a piece of beef weighing

a) 3 kg?   **b)** 8 kg?

c) $5\frac{1}{2}$ kg?   **d)** 3·2 kg?

6 The cost, in pounds, of hiring a car is the number of days multiplied by 18.
Find the cost to hire the car for

a) 3 days.   **b)** 14 days.

7 To find how much you earn an hour, divide the total pay by the number of hours worked.
Find the hourly pay if

a) the total pay is £200 and you worked 40 hours.

b) the total pay is £234 and you worked 36 hours.

8 The speed of a car in kilometres per hour is 3600 divided by the time, in seconds, it takes to cover 1 kilometre.
Find the speed when the time is

a) 30 seconds.   **b)** 50 seconds.

9 The area of a triangle is the length of the base multiplied by the height divided by two.
Find the area of a triangle with

a) height 4 cm and base 6 cm.

b) height 3·2 cm and base 7 cm.

10 The cost of an item in euros is the cost in pounds times 1·6.
Find the cost in euros of an item costing

a) £10.   **b)** £37.

EXERCISE 4.2H

1 An approximate formula for finding the circumference of a circle is $C = 3d$, where d is the diameter.
Find C when

a) $d = 2$ m.

b) $d = 5 \cdot 7$ m.

2 One formula to find the perimeter of a rectangle is $P = 2a + 2b$, where a is the length and b is the width.
Find P when

a) $a = 5$ cm and $b = 6$ cm.

b) $a = 2 \cdot 7$ cm and $b = 1 \cdot 9$ cm.

3 The formula $M = 75 - 3s$ represents the number of matches, M, remaining in a pattern when a number of shapes, s, is taken away.
Find M when

a) $s = 1$.

b) $s = 4$.

4 A formula for finding the amount of money raised by a runner in a sponsored run is £$X = 5k + 2$, where X is the amount raised and k is the distance run.
Find X when

a) $k = 10$

b) $k = 42 \cdot 2$.

5 The formula for working out the weight in grams of dessert remaining in a serving bowl is
$R = 3000 - ps$, where p is the number of portions taken out and s is the weight in grams of each portion.
Find R when

a) $p = 2$ and $s = 150$.

b) $p = 7$ and $s = 175$.

Working with measures

EXERCISE 5.1H

1 Change these capacities to millilitres.
  a) 8 litres   **b)** 0·70 litres
  c) 9·02 litres   **d)** 25 cl
  e) 8·6 cl

2 Change these capacities to litres.
  a) 6800 ml   **b)** 90 ml   **c)** 707 ml
  d) 47 cl   **e)** 5·67 cl

3 Write these capacities in order of size, smallest first.
670 ml, 5·4 litres, 43·9 cl, 0·39 litres, 82 cl

STAG

3

4 A bottle of wine holds 700 ml.
A waiter pours 225 ml into a glass.
How much wine is left in the bottle?

5 A large container holds 2·5 litres of shampoo.
125 ml of shampoo is spilled from the container.
How much shampoo is left?

EXERCISE 5.2H

1 Estimate these in metric units.

  a) The mass of a litre bottle of water

  b) The diameter of a wheel on a bus

  c) The height of your desk

  d) The capacity of a garden watering can

  e) The height of a two-storey house

2 Estimate

  a) the height of the bus.

  b) the length of the bus.

3 The car is 3·6 metres long.
Estimate the length of the train.

4 The car is 4·2 metres long. Estimate

  a) the height of the aircraft.

  b) the length of the aircraft.

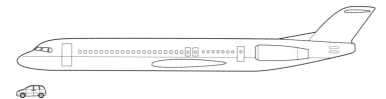

EXERCISE 5.3H

1 Read the points marked A, B and C on this scale.

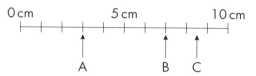

2 Read this scale.

3 Read the points marked A and B on this thermometer.

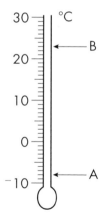

4 How long is this nail?

5 Measure the distance between A and B.

6 Read the points marked with letters on these scales.

a)

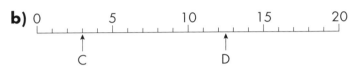

b)

c)

d)

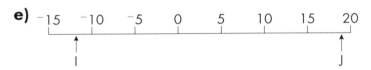

e) ⁻15 ⁻10 ⁻5 0 5 10 15 20

I   J

Fractions

1 Find $\frac{1}{2}$ of 86.

2 Find $\frac{1}{5}$ of 75.

3 Find $\frac{1}{3}$ of 48.

4 Find $\frac{1}{4}$ of 120.

5 There are 973 students in a school.
$\frac{1}{7}$ of them are left-handed.
How many students in the school are left-handed?

6 A shop has a '$\frac{1}{3}$ off everything' sale.
A CD player normally costs £198.
How much does it cost in the sale?

STAG

3

15

1 Find $\frac{3}{7}$ of 196.

2 Find $\frac{5}{9}$ of 666.

3 Find $\frac{7}{8}$ of 192.

4 Find $\frac{4}{11}$ of 572.

5 Find $\frac{3}{5}$ of 235.

6 Find $\frac{4}{7}$ of 357.

7 Find $\frac{5}{8}$ of 432.

8 Find $\frac{5}{6}$ of 876.

9 Which is larger, a $\frac{3}{8}$ share of £240 or a
$\frac{3}{5}$ share of £150?
Show your working.

10 Harry opened a packet of Liquorice Allsorts and
found that it contained 40 sweets.
$\frac{1}{5}$ of the sweets were plain liquorice and $\frac{3}{5}$ of the
sweets were pink.
How many sweets were

a) plain liquorice?

b) pink?

11 A family received a water bill for £84·40.
$\frac{3}{8}$ of the amount of the bill was for a 'standing charge'.
How much was the standing charge?

Probability

EXERCISE 7.1H

1 When you throw a fair dice, find the probability of getting

a) an odd number.

b) a five.

c) a seven.

2 When you throw a fair dice, find the probability of getting a number 4 or less.

3 There are 7 white balls and 8 red balls in a bag.
You take one out without looking.
What is the probability that it is

a) red?

b) white?

c) blue?

4 A letter is chosen at random from the word EXCELLENT.
What is the probability that it is

a) an E?

b) a consonant?

5 One hundred and fifty tickets are sold for a raffle.
You buy one ticket.
What is the probability that you will win?

STAG
3

6 Belle has ten pens.
Three are black, five are blue and two are red.
Belle chooses one pen without looking.
What is the probability that the pen is

a) red?

b) black?

c) not blue?

7 There are 30 balls in a bag, nine of them are blue
and eight of them are yellow.
You take one out without looking.
What is the probability that it is

a) blue?

b) yellow?

c) neither blue or yellow?

8 A letter is chosen at random from the word
PROBABILITY.
What is the probability that it is

a) an A?   **b)** an I?   **c)** an X?

9 A card game uses a standard pack of playing cards.
One card is selected at random.
What is the probability that the card will be

a) black?

b) a king?

c) a 'picture' card?

10 There are 72 counters in a bag, 27 of them are blue,
15 are yellow, 12 are green and the rest are red.
You take one counter from the bag without looking.
What is the probability that the counter chosen is

a) green?   **b)** yellow?

c) not blue?   **d)** red?

Using graphs

EXERCISE 8.1H

1 The table shows the distances in kilometres an aircraft flies in given times.

Time (h)	Distance (km)
0	0
2	1500
4	3000
8	6000

a) Plot the points on a graph.
Put time on the horizontal axis with a scale of 1 cm to 1 hour.
Put distance on the vertical axis with a scale of 1 cm to 1000 km.
Join the points with a straight line.

b) Find the distance travelled after
   (i) 5 hours.
   (ii) $1\frac{1}{2}$ hours.

c) Find the time taken to travel
   (i) 1000 km.
   (ii) 5500 km.

STAG
3

2 This conversion graph is for euros (€) to dollars ($) for amounts up to €100.

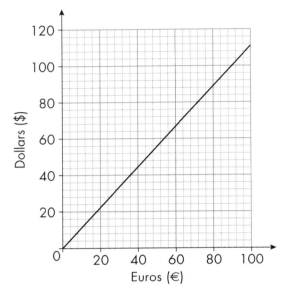

Use the graph to find

a) the number of dollars equal to
   (i) €50.
   (ii) €85.

b) the number of euros equal to
   (i) $100.
   (ii) $35.

c) How many dollars are equal to €150?

3 This conversion graph is for centimetres to inches.

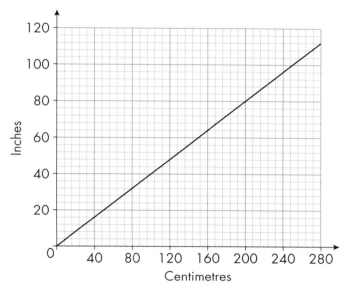

Use the graph to find

a) the number of inches equal to
  (i) 100 cm.   **(ii)** 168 cm.

b) the number of centimetres equal to
  (i) 50 inches.   **(ii)** 21 inches.

c) How many centimetres are equal to 200 inches?

4 a) On a piece of graph paper, mark axes horizontally for pounds (£) up to £100, using 1 cm to £10, and vertically for dollars ($) up to $160, using 1 cm to $20.

b) Plot the point (100, 142) and join it to (0, 0) with a straight line.

c) Find the number of dollars equal to
  (i) £50.   **(ii)** £85.

d) Find the number of pounds equal to
  (i) $100.   **(ii)** $53.

e) How many dollars are equal to £1?

5 Area of land used to be measured in acres.
It is now measured in hectares (ha).
One hectare is 10 000 m².
This conversion graph is for acres to hectares, up to 200 acres.

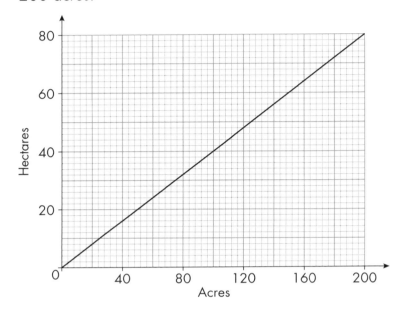

Use the graph to find how many

a) hectares is 100 acres.

b) acres is 45 ha.

c) acres is 1 ha.

Equations

9

pt

In questions **1** to **20**, solve the equations.

1 $4a = 48$

2 $2b = 38$

3 $5c = 30$

4 $d + 3 = 7$

5 $e + 7 = 11$

6 $f + 15 = 16$

7 $g - 7 = 3$

8 $4 + h = 13$

9 $2j = 23$

10 $k \div 3 = 6$

11 $7m = 91$

12 $5n = 4$

13 $25 = 32 - p$

14 $q - 6 = 17$

15 $r + 23 = 52$

16 $s \div 25 = 8$

STAG
3

23

17 $t - 3 = 6$

18 $u + 7 = 3$

19 $15 + v = 10$

20 $8 - w = 10$

21 Marie-Jo has a collection of 15 soft toys that cost a total of £60.

   a) If c is the cost of a soft toy, write down an equation with c in it for the cost of one soft toy.

   b) Solve the equation in part **a)** to find the cost of one soft toy.

22 Before being cooked a chicken weighed 4·3 kg. During cooking the chicken lost 0·8 kg in weight.

   a) If the chicken weighed w kg after cooking, write down an equation with w in it.

   b) Solve the equation in part **a)** to find the weight of the chicken after cooking.

Mean and range 10

1 These are the wingspans, in centimetres, of some birds.

21   27   19   23   25   22   25   26

Find the mean and range.

2 Twelve peapods were picked and the number of peas in each were counted.

8   12   5   11   12   10
13   7   8   9   7   6

Find the mean and range.

3 The numbers of sweets in ten tubes were counted.

31   29   32   32   25
33   31   30   34   28

Find the mean and range.

4 Find the mean and range of this set of data.

3   6   5   4   7   6   8   1

5 These are the heights of a collection of plants.

50 cm   65 cm   80 cm   40 cm   35 cm

Find the mean and range of these heights.

STAG
3

25

6 These are the marks some students scored in a test.

9   7   8   7   5   6   8   9   5   6

Find the mean and range of these marks.

7 These are the ages of a group of friends.

18   22   21   19   18   18   17   19   17   21

Find the mean and range of these ages.

8 These are the salaries of ten workers in a small company.

£20 000   £20 000   £20 000   £18 000
£22 000   £23 000   £25 000   £21 000
£23 000   £28 000

Find the mean and range of these salaries.

Percentages

11

1 Find 10% of £50.

2 Find 10% of £7·50.

3 Find 30% of £150.

4 Find 20% of £85.

5 Find 30% of £7·20.

6 Find 5% of £6·80.

7 Find 20% of £1·20.

8 Find 5% of £850.

9 Find 15% of £40.

10 Find 15% of £175.

11 Find 10% of £83.

12 Find 10% of £246.

13 Find 20% of £270.

14 Find 25% of £162.

15 Find 30% of £12·60.

16 Find 40% of £1·70.

17 Find 75% of £56.

STAGE
3

18 Find 35% of £180.

19 Find 45% of £240.

20 Find 85% of £160.

21 65% of the 840 students in a school eat in the cafeteria.
How many students is this?

22 An office manager found that 5% of the paper used for photocopying was wasted.
On one day the total number of photocopies made was 620.
How many copies were wasted?

23 The Green family recycle all paper from their household.
One month 45% of the weight of paper recycled was from magazines and newspapers.
If the family recycled 60 kg of paper, what was the weight of magazines and newspapers?

24 One month a family spent 15% of their income on entertainment.
If they had a total income of £2300, how much was spent on entertainment?

25 35% of the contents of a packet of crisps are fat.
There are 32 grams of crisps in a packet.
What is the weight of fat in a packet of crisps?

Three-dimensional shapes

▌▐▌▌▌ EXERCISE 12.1H

1 a) Draw this shape, putting in the hidden edges as dashed lines.

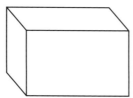

b) What are the shapes of the faces of a cuboid?

2 a) Draw this shape, putting in the hidden edges as dashed lines.

b) What are the shapes of the faces of the prism?

3 a) Draw this shape, putting in the hidden edges as dashed lines.

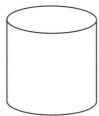

b) What is the shape of the top of the cylinder?

Three-dimensional shapes

1 These are the views of a solid shape from the front, the side and above.

Which of these shapes are the views of?

1

4

2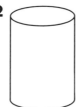

5

3

6

AGE
3

2 Look at this picture of children on a see-saw.

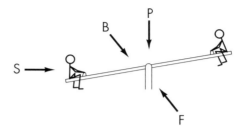

a) These pictures show the children on the see-saw viewed from three of the different positions shown with arrows.

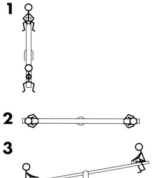

Match each view with the correct letter.

b) Sketch the view of just the see-saw from the position marked B.

STA

EXERCISE 12.3H

Draw these shapes on triangle spotty paper.
Make sure the paper is the correct way round.

1

2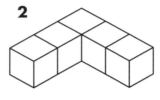

3

4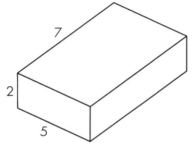

5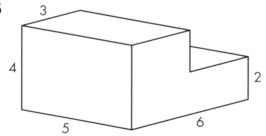

6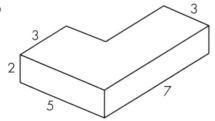

Collecting and illustrating data

EXERCISE 13.1H

1 These are the numbers of matches in 50 boxes.

47 49 46 46 49 47 48 45 51 47
46 46 51 48 47 50 49 50 48 46
50 49 47 49 51 46 48 46 47 46
47 48 46 50 49 48 47 47 49 47
46 50 47 47 49 47 49 46 47 48

a) Make a frequency table and record the totals.

b) Draw a bar chart to show this information.

c) How many boxes contained 50 matches?

2 These are the numbers of hours Mr Smith worked each day last month.

5 6 9   5   7 5 11 11   9 8 6 5
8 8 9 10 10 8   8   8 10 8 9 5

a) Make a frequency table and record the totals.

b) Show this information on a vertical line graph.

c) What was the most common number of hours that Mr Smith worked?

STAG
3

3 This table shows the number of cars at each house in a road.

Number of cars	0	1	2	3	4
Number of houses	2	12	15	0	1

Show this information on a bar chart.

4 Draw a vertical line graph to show each of these sets of data.

a)

Type of fast food	Frequency
Pizza	18
Chinese	8
Burger	13
Kebab	6
Fish and chips	4
Other	25

b)

Type of vehicle	Frequency
Car	43
Van	29
Lorry	15
Bus	7
Motorbike	4
Other	2

c)

Type of tree	Frequency
Oak	3
Beech	7
Pine	10
Sycamore	6
Lime	2
Other	2

5 Draw a bar chart to show each of these sets of data.

a)

Favourite colour	Frequency
Blue	23
Red	9
Green	6
Yellow	4
Pink	7
Black	3
Other	8

b)

Shoe size	Frequency
39	12
40	8
41	15
42	11
43	9
44	6
45	2
Other	7

STA

c)

Number of sisters	Frequency
0	7
1	12
2	8
3	2
4 or more	1

6 Emily did a survey of the birds landing in her garden during one week.
Her results are shown in this bar chart.

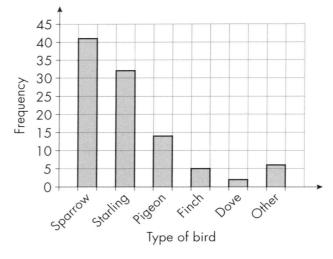

a) How many pigeons landed in Emily's garden?

b) What type of bird was the least common?

c) How many birds in total landed in Emily's garden?

7 Siobhan did a survey of the number of glasses of water people in her year drank in one day. Her results are shown in this bar chart.

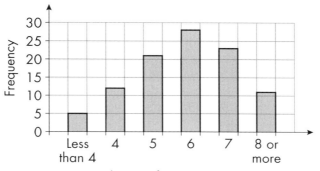

Glasses of water per day

a) How many people were in the survey?

b) How many people drank eight or more glasses of water in a day?

c) What is the most common number of glasses of water drunk in a day by people in this survey?

8 This vertical line graph shows the number of pets kept by each of a group of people.

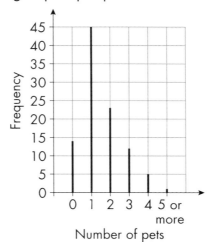

Number of pets

a) How many people in the survey did not have pets?

b) How many people had only one pet?

c) How many people had three or more pets?

STA

Order of operations

14

EXERCISE 14.1H

Work out these.

Do not use a calculator for question **1**.

1 a) $4 + 7 \times 2$

   b) $3 \times 4 - 2$

   c) $(12 - 3) \times 3$

You may use your calculator for questions **2** to **8**.

2 a) $(7 \cdot 3 + 3 \cdot 2) \div 4 \cdot 8$

   b) $(134 - 43) \div 35$

   c) $(8 \cdot 2 - 3 \cdot 6) \times 5 \cdot 4$

3 a) $\dfrac{6 \cdot 8}{1 \cdot 3 + 2 \cdot 1}$

   b) $\dfrac{46 \times 13}{65}$

   c) $\dfrac{53 - 24}{58}$

4 a) $6 \cdot 4 + 10 \cdot 3 \times 12$

   b) $13 \times (7 \cdot 6 - 4 \cdot 3)$

   c) $13 \times 7 \cdot 6 - 4 \cdot 3$

5 a) $25 \cdot 7 + \dfrac{1 \cdot 96}{4 \cdot 9}$

b) $\dfrac{25 \cdot 7 + 19 \cdot 6}{15 \cdot 1}$

c) $\dfrac{18 \cdot 2 - 11 \cdot 8}{10 \cdot 7 - 7 \cdot 5}$

6 a) $(11 \cdot 2 + 6 \cdot 4) \div 8 - 2$

b) $72 - (5 \cdot 9 \times 4) + 1 \cdot 6$

c) $8 - 4 \times (0 \cdot 3 + 1 \cdot 9) + 5$

7 a) $\dfrac{5 \cdot 2}{6 \cdot 5} + \dfrac{6 \cdot 5}{5 \cdot 2}$

b) $\dfrac{6 \cdot 8}{0 \cdot 85} - \dfrac{8 \cdot 5}{34}$

c) $\dfrac{11 \cdot 5}{7 \cdot 4 + 1 \cdot 8} + \dfrac{0 \cdot 4}{0 \cdot 25}$

8 a) $4 \cdot 7^2 + 7 \cdot 2^2$

b) $3 \cdot 4^2 - 2 \cdot 7^2$

c) $9 \cdot 2 - 3 \cdot 6 \times 2 \cdot 3$

STA

15 Scale drawings

EXERCISE 15.1H pt

1 Measure each of these lines as accurately as possible.
Using the scales given, work out the length that each line represents.

a) ————————————————

Scale: 1 cm to 6 m

b) ———————————

Scale: 1 cm to 20 km

c) ————————————————————

Scale: 2 cm to 5 miles

d) ———————————

Scale: 1 cm to 4 m

2 Draw accurately the line to represent these actual lengths.
Use the scale given.

a) 6 m   Scale: 1 cm to 1 m

b) 8 km   Scale: 1 cm to 2 km

c) 15 miles   Scale: 3 cm to 5 miles

d) 450 m   Scale: 1 cm to 100 m

3 Here is the plan of an office.
The scale is 2 cm to 1 m.

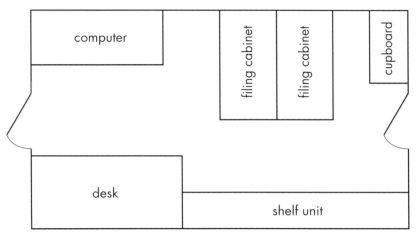

Find the real length and width of

a) the whole office.　　　　**b)** the filing cabinets.

c) the shelf unit.　　　　　**d)** the desk.

4 Here is a map of part of Belgium.
The scale of the map is 1 cm to 30 km.

How far is it, in kilometres, from

a) Ostend to Liège?　　　　**b)** Antwerp to Mons?

STA

5 Here is a plan of a bedroom.
The scale of the diagram is 1 cm to 50 cm.

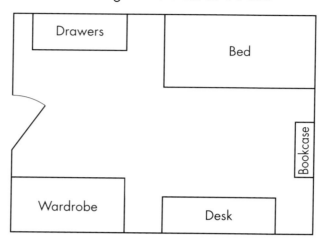

a) Work out the length and width of the bedroom.

b) Work out the length and width of each of the five items in the bedroom.

c) The window in the bedroom measures 1 m by 1 m 75 cm.
What will the measurements of the window be on this scale drawing?

6 The map opposite shows some towns and cities in Scotland.
The scale of the map is 1 cm to 10 km.

a) What is the real distance, in kilometres, between these towns?

   (i)   Glasgow and Stirling
   (ii) Edinburgh and Glasgow
   (iii) Edinburgh and Perth
   (iv) Glasgow and Dundee
   (v) Perth and Dundee
   (vi) Edinburgh and Stirling

b) It is 660 km from Edinburgh to London.
How many centimetres would this be on the map?

Dundee

Perth

Firth of Forth

Edinburgh

Stirling

Glasgow

Scale: 1 cm = 10 km

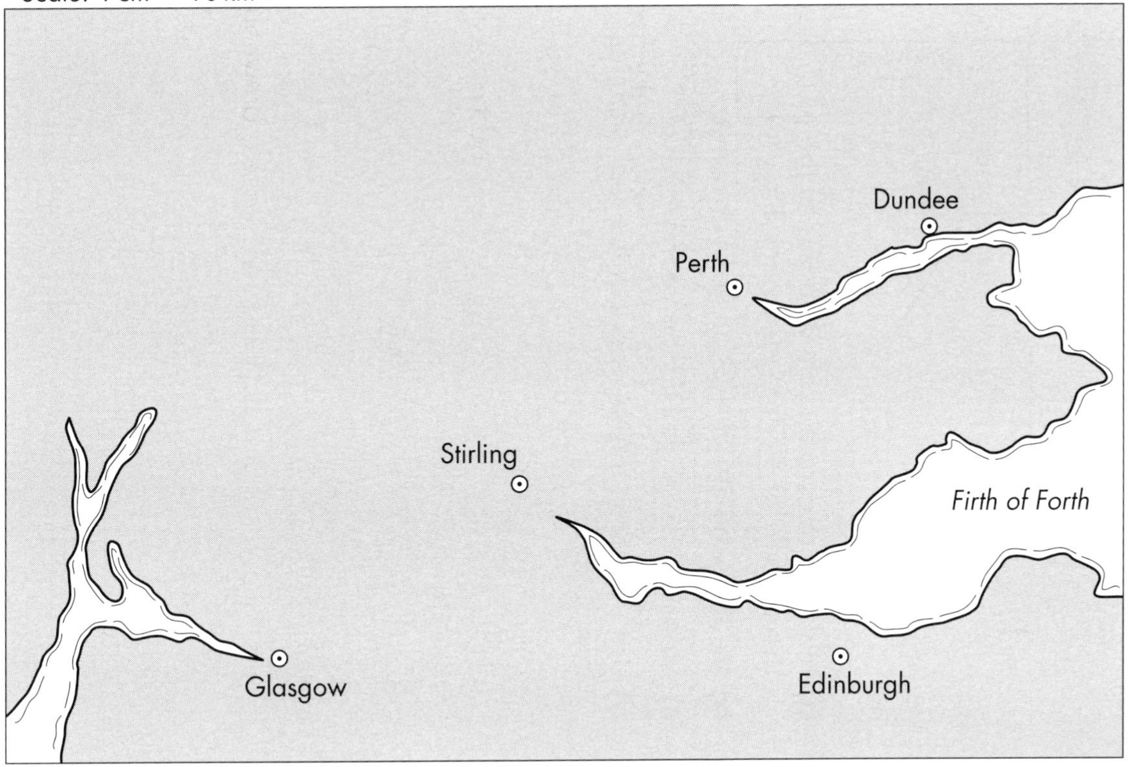

7 The sketch shows a plan of a play area.

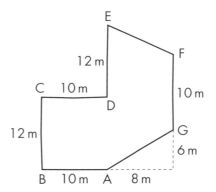

a) Make an accurate scale drawing of the play area. Use a scale of 1 cm to represent 2 m.

b) Measure the length AG on your drawing.

c) Measure the angle DEF on your drawing.

d) Use your drawing to work out the real distance from C to G.

Enlargement

EXERCISE 16.1H

1 For each of these shapes, copy the shape on to squared paper and draw an enlargement using the scale factor given.

a) Scale factor 2

b) Scale factor 3

c) Scale factor 3

d) Scale factor 2

e) Scale factor 3

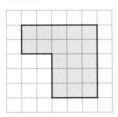

f) Scale factor 2

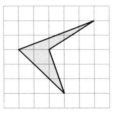

g) Scale factor 2

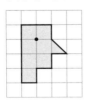

h) Scale factor 4

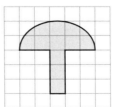

STAG

3

2 Measure the lengths in the two shapes to see if one is an enlargement of the other.
If so, say how many times larger it is.

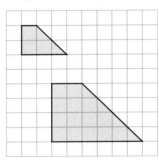

3 Which of these diagrams show one shape as a 3 times enlargement of the other?

a)

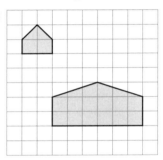

b)

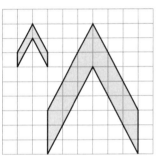

Stage 4 Contents

STAG

4

Decimals, fractions and percentages

EXERCISE 1.1H

1 What does the 4 represent in each of these numbers?

a) 74   **b)** 415

c) 20·43   **d)** 8425

e) 61·24   **f)** 42·13

g) 0·004   **h)** 64 200 000

2 Write these decimals as fractions.

a) 0·7   **b)** 0·83

c) 0·25   **d)** 0·507

e) 0·09   **f)** 0·4

g) 3·01   **h)** 0·013

3 Write these fractions as decimals.

a) $\frac{3}{5}$ **b)** $\frac{14}{100}$ **c)** $2\frac{3}{4}$ **d)** $1\frac{7}{10}$

e) $35\frac{1}{100}$ **f)** $6\frac{13}{100}$ **g)** $\frac{7}{1000}$ **h)** $5\frac{99}{100}$

4 Write these as decimals or whole numbers.

a) four and one tenth

b) three million, eight hundred thousand and sixty-two

c) eighteen thousandths

d) seventy-two and seven hundredths

e) nine thousand, four hundred and one and three tenths

STAG

4

1 Put these whole numbers in order of size, smallest first.

a) 782, 2807, 1872, 287, 87, 708

b) 439, 3047, 8372, 48, 843, 4389

c) 1260, 10 086, 80 060, 100 000, 806

2 Put these decimals in order of size, smallest first.

a) 0·29, 0·902, 0·249, 0·9402, 0·021

b) 0·803, 0·083, 0·0083, 0·003 08, 0·38

c) 0·092, 0·409, 0·429, 0·0942, 0·9

3 Put these numbers in order of size, smallest first.

a) 83·1, 4270, 0·92, 6·347, 762·53

b) 3·01, 0·103, 13·01, 1·003, 3100

c) 17·24, 70·14, 1472, 4·017, 0·741

4 Here are five digits: 5, 1, 6, 4, 8.
Using each digit only once, write down

a) the smallest whole number that can be made with the five digits.

b) the largest whole number that can be made with the five digits.

5 Put these in order, smallest first.

a) 0·33, $\frac{31}{100}$, $\frac{29}{100}$, 0·3, 0·32

b) 0·55, $\frac{57}{100}$, $\frac{56}{100}$, 0·5, 0·54

c) $3\frac{71}{100}$, 3·73, $3\frac{7}{10}$, 3·78, 3·8

d) $8\frac{43}{100}$, $8\frac{4}{10}$, 8·4, 8·47, 8·39

e) 0·25, $\frac{3}{10}$, $\frac{28}{100}$, 0·35, 0·27

f) 0·46, $\frac{64}{100}$, $\frac{56}{100}$, 0·45, 0·65

EXERCISE 1.3H

1 Work out these.

a) $\frac{1}{5}$ of 45   **b)** $\frac{1}{4}$ of 48

c) $\frac{2}{5}$ of 40   **d)** $\frac{3}{10}$ of 180

e) $\frac{5}{8}$ of 48   **f)** $\frac{7}{10}$ of 130

g) $\frac{3}{8}$ of 72   **h)** $\frac{3}{4}$ of 220

2 Change these fractions to percentages.

a) $\frac{1}{5}$ **b)** $\frac{1}{4}$ **c)** $\frac{4}{5}$ **d)** $\frac{9}{10}$

e) $\frac{3}{10}$ **f)** $\frac{7}{10}$ **g)** $\frac{3}{4}$ **h)** $\frac{3}{5}$

3 Work out these.

a) 20% of £30   **b)** 25% of £28

c) 60% of £170   **d)** 5% of 80 m

e) 75% of 432 m   **f)** 30% of £46

g) 15% of 34 m   **h)** 40% of 230 m

4 A class has 30 students.
Two fifths of the class are girls.

a) What percentage of the class are girls?

b) How many girls are there in the class?

5 A pair of jeans at £55 was reduced by 20% in a sale.

a) How much is the reduction?

b) What was the sale price?

6 A TV licence used to cost £140.
The price was increased by 5%.

a) How much is the increase?

b) What is the new price of a TV licence?

2 Coordinates

You may find the example useful for both of these exercises.

EXERCISE 2.1H

1 Write down the coordinates of the points A to G.

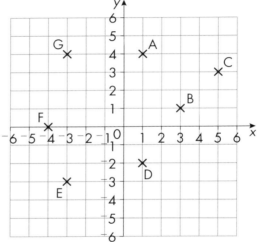

2 On squared paper, draw and label axes from ⁻5 to 5 for both x and y.
Plot these points.
A(1, 3) B(4, 1) C(5, 0) D(⁻2, 4)
E(⁻4, 1) F(⁻4, ⁻5) G(2, ⁻2) H(0, ⁻5)

3 On squared paper, draw and label axes from 0 to 5 for both x and y.
Plot these points to make a number.
Plot A(1, 5), B(1, 2) and C(3, 2).
Join A to B to C.
Plot D(2, 3) and E(2, 1). Join D to E.

EXERCISE 2.2H

1 On squared paper, draw and label axes from ⁻5 to 5 for both x and y.

a) Plot and label these points on the graph.
A(⁻4, 1)   B(⁻1, 4)   C(5, 1)   D(⁻1, ⁻2)
Join the points to form the shape ABCD.

b) What is this shape called?

2 On squared paper, draw and label axes from ⁻5 to 5 for both x and y.

a) Plot and label these points on the graph.
A(2, 4)   B(2, ⁻2)   C(⁻1, ⁻4)   D(⁻1, 2)
Join the points to form the shape ABCD.

b) What is the special name of this shape?

3 On squared paper, draw and label axes from ⁻5 to 5 for both x and y.

a) Plot and label these points on the graph.
A(2, 2)   B(5, ⁻3)   C(⁻1, ⁻3)   D(⁻2, 2)
Join the points to form the shape ABCD.

b) What is the special name of this shape?

4 On squared paper, draw and label axes from ⁻5 to 5 for both x and y.

a) Plot and label these points on the graph.
A(⁻2, 5)   B(3, 2)   C(0, ⁻3)

b) Mark the point D on the graph so that ABCD is a square.

c) Write down the coordinates of D.

5 On squared paper, draw and label axes from ⁻5 to 5 for both x and y.

a) Plot and label A(⁻5, 4) and B(3, ⁻4).

b) Join the points and mark the midpoint.

c) Write down the coordinates of the midpoint of AB.

6 Plot and label the points A(1, 3), B(1, ⁻4) and C(⁻3, ⁻4).
Mark the point D so that ABCD is a rectangle.
Write down the coordinates of D.

7 Plot and label the points A(1, 1), B(5, ⁻1) and D(⁻3, ⁻1).
Mark the point C so that ABCD is a rhombus.
Write down the coordinates of C.

8 Plot and label the points A(⁻1, 4), B(1, 0) and C(⁻3, ⁻2).
Mark the point D so that ABCD is a square.
Write down the coordinates of D.

9 Plot and label the points A(⁻2, 2), B(3, 3) and C(1, ⁻2).
Mark the point D so that ABCD is a parallelogram.
Write down the coordinates of D.

AGE
4

Sequences

EXERCISE 3.1H pt

1 Write down the next three terms in each of these sequences

a) 7, 10, 13, 16, …, …, …

b) 87, 80, 73, 66, …, …, …

c) 0·2, 0·4, 0·6, 0·8, …, …, …

d) 1, 8, 15, 22, 29, 36, …, …, …

e) 7, 13, 19, 25, 31, 37, …, …, …

f) 9, 17, 25, 33, 41, 49, …, …, …

g) 4, 13, 22, 31, 40, 49, …, …, …

h) 16, 21, 26, 31, 36, 41, …, …, …

2 Here are four patterns of sticks.

Pattern 1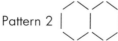

Pattern 2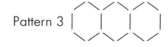

Pattern 3

Pattern 4

a) Draw the next two patterns.

b) Write down the first six terms of the sequence of the number of sticks.

STAG

4

3 In each part of this question, draw the next pattern and write down the number of lines in each of the first six patterns.

a)

b)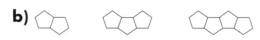

c)

4 Here are three patterns of tiles.

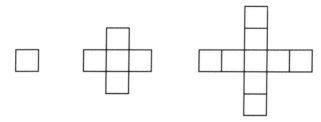

a) Draw the next two patterns.

b) Copy and complete this table.

Pattern	1	2	3	4	5
Squares					

5 Here are three patterns of squares and crosses.

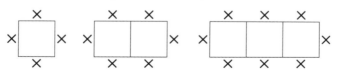

a) Draw the next two patterns.

b) Copy and complete this table.

Squares	1	2	3	4	5
Crosses					

EXERCISE 3.2H

1 Write down the first four terms of each of these sequences.

a) Starts with 3 and 3 is added each time.

b) Starts with 26 and 2 is subtracted each time.

c) Starts with 1 and it is multiplied by 10 each time.

d) Starts with 5 and 4 is added each time.

e) Starts with 1000 and it is divided by 10 each time.

f) Starts with 12 and it is halved each time.

2 For each of these sequences, find a term-to-term rule and write down the next three terms.

a) 3	6	9	12
b) 100	99	98	97
c) 1	2	4	8
d) 6	5·5	5	4·5
e) 29	23	17	11
f) 25	18	11	4
g) 16	11	6	1
h) 17	11	5	$^-1$
i) 27	19	11	3
j) 42	29	16	3
k) 5	9	13	17
l) 22	17	12	7
m) 10	100	1000	10 000
n) 24	12	6	3

3 Find the missing numbers in each of these sequences. For each sequence, write down the term-to-term rule that connects the numbers.

a) 1, 7, ..., 19, 25, ...

b) 11, ..., 35, 47, ..., 71

c) 85, ..., 67, ..., 49, 40

d) ..., 87, 83, 79, ..., 71

e) 7, 22, ..., ..., 67, 82

f) 34, ..., 20, 13, 6, ...

▌▐‖ EXERCISE 3.3H

1 Write down the first five terms of the sequences with these nth terms.

a) $7n - 3$

b) $9n - 6$

c) $13n - 11$

d) $2n + 61$

e) $4n + 39$

f) $3n + 13$

2 Find the 100th term of the sequences with these nth terms.

a) $4n + 4$

b) $3n + 34$

c) $13n - 8$

d) $9n - 1$

e) $5n + 38$

f) $6n + 19$

Solving problems 1

4

EXERCISE 4.1H

pt

1 This table shows the cost of posting some airmail letters.

Weight not over	Europe	World Zone 1	World Zone 2
20 g	£0·36	£0·65	£0·65
40 g	£0·50	£1·00	£1·07
60 g	£0·65	£1·35	£1·49

Kate posts a letter weighing 32 g to Europe and a letter weighing 55 g to Australia, which is in World Zone 2.
How much does she have to pay altogether?

2 This table shows the distances in miles between four towns in Derbyshire.

Bakewell			
12	Buxton		
13	29	Chesterfield	
8	20	9	Matlock

Christine travels from Buxton to Matlock and then from Matlock to Bakewell.
How many miles does she travel?

STAG
4

Solving problems

3 The Patel family of two adults and three children went to the cinema.
How much did their tickets cost?

Cinema Tickets	
Adults	£6·50
Children	£4

4 David wants 8 litres of lemonade for a party.
How much does he have to pay, with this special offer?

Buy 1 get 1 free!
2-litre bottles of Lemonade
only **99p**

5 On holiday in France, Jason made this table of approximate conversions between kilometres per hour (km/h) and miles per hour (mph).

km/h	40	50	60	70	80	90	100	110	120
mph	25	30	40	45	50	55	60	65	75

A more accurate conversion is mph = km/h × 0·625.

a) Jason saw a speed limit sign of 90 km/h.
What is the speed limit in mph
(i) according to his table?
(ii) using the more accurate conversion?

b) Some of the conversions in the table are exactly the same as using the accurate conversion. List them.

6 The table shows the cost per minute, in pence, of phone calls to various parts of the world.

Country	Price per minute (pence)	Country	Price per minute (pence)
Australia	3·5	New Zealand	4·16
Canada	4·16	Pakistan	16·66
China	3	Philippines	14·18
France	3·5	Poland	3·5
Germany	3·5	Russia	5
Hungary	4·5	South Africa	6
India	12·5	Spain	3·5
Ireland	3·5	Thailand	7·5
Italy	3·5	UK	3·5
Jamaica	7·5	United States	3·5
Lithuania	9	Zimbabwe	6·5

a) How much does a 10-minute call to Spain cost?

b) Which other countries cost the same to phone as France?

c) Selina wants to phone her cousin in South Africa. She has only £1 to spend.
What is the greatest number of complete minutes she can phone for?

EXERCISE 4.2H

1 a) Joanne bought three pizzas at £2·79 each.
How much did they cost?

b) Joanne paid for the pizzas with a £10 note.
How much change did she get?

2 a) Ali bought five colas and spent £3·75.
How much was each cola?

b) Ali paid for the colas with a £5 note.
How much change did he get?

3 Peter opened a 500 g bag of dried pasta.
He cooked for four people, using 75 g of pasta per person.
How much pasta was left in the bag?

4 Melissa used 480 g of rice for a meal for six people.
How much rice did she use for each person?

5 Carla potted some geraniums.
For each pot she needed 0·2 litres of compost.
How many pots could she fill from a 10-litre bag of compost?

6 Claude was fixing fence posts in his garden.
He used 25 kg of concrete to fix each post.
How much concrete did he need to fix 30 fence posts?

7 John cycles to and from school each day.
He lives 2·4 miles from the school.
One weekend he cycled 17·6 miles.
How many miles did he cycle altogether that week?

8 Nadine runs 8 km each day from Monday to Friday.
She runs 15 km on a Saturday and a total of 60 km in the week.
What distance does she run on a Sunday?

9 One week, Jean used her car for long journeys of 220 miles and 176 miles.
At the beginning of the week her milometer showed 17 659.
At the end of the week it showed 18 137.
For how many miles did she use her car for short journeys that week?

10 At the bakers, Joe bought four jam doughnuts costing 35p each and two Cornish pasties.
He gave the assistant £5 and got £1·70 change.
How much did each Cornish pasty cost?

11 At the greengrocers, Malik bought four oranges costing 30p each, some bananas costing £1·08 and three grapefruit. He paid with a £5 note and was given £1·37 in change.
How much did each grapefruit cost?

12 On his holidays, James calculates that he travelled a total of 14 020 km.
He knows that he flew 11 450 km and that he drove 2365 km.
He used public transport for all his other journeys.
What distance did he travel using public transport?

STA

5 Averages and range

1 These are the numbers of goals scored by Catherine and Mandy in ten netball matches.

Catherine

6 5 2 1 4 3 1 2 8 7

Mandy

4 3 2 2 0 1 5 4 9 6

a) Work out the mean, median and range for each girl.

b) Compare the number of goals they each scored.

2 Two varieties of tomato plants were grown, ten of each variety.
Here are their heights in centimetres, five weeks after sowing.

Variety A

7 11 8 10 12 11 9 8 10 10

Variety B

8 12 7 6 11 10 7 12 11 10

a) Work out the mean, median and range for each variety.

b) Compare the heights of the two varieties.

3 These are the handspans in centimetres of ten students in each of two classes.

Class R

20 18 17 18 19 21 20 22 20 19

Class S

20 18 17 16 18 19 15 18 17 16

a) Work out the mean, median and range for each class.

b) Compare the handspans of the two groups.

4 These are the water bills, per year, of the 15 families in one village.

£450 £410 £250 £190 £675
£390 £270 £435 £370 £430
£415 £430 £420 £365 £305

It was claimed that 'the average water bill is more than £400 a year'. Comment on this statement.

STA

5 These diagrams show the performances of boys and girls in a general knowledge test.

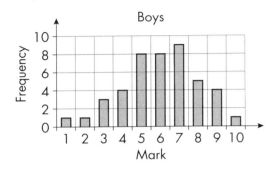

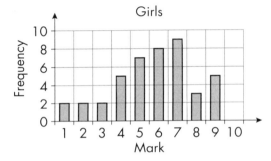

a) How many girls scored 7 in the test?

b) How many boys scored 4 in the test?

c) What was the modal score for the girls?

d) What was the modal score for the boys?

e) What was the range of the scores for the girls?

f) Did girls or boys do better in this test?
Give a reason for your answer.

Working without a calculator

EXERCISE 6.1H

1 Work out these.

a) £3·35
   +£4·14

b) £6·56
   +£3·03

c) £8·27
   +£1·68

d) £5·43
   +£3·29

e) £8·15
   +£9·47

f) £7·69
   +£4·75

g) £34·80
   −£2·40

h) £9·58
   −£6·66

i) £8·25
   −£3·07

j) £10·70
   −£7·45

k) £14·45
   −£8·38

l) £20·00
   −£4·98

2 Work out these.

a) £3·54 + 97p

b) £18·50 − 949p

c) £105 − £27·49

d) 67p + £4·28

e) £1·50 − 69p

f) £7 − £3·89

STAG

4

3 Work out these.

   a) $7 \cdot 6$ m $+ 2 \cdot 1$ m

   b) 3 m $+ 6$ m 90 cm

   c) 4 m 37 cm $+ 5$ m 88 cm

   d) 5 m $+ 345$ cm

   e) $7 \cdot 3$ m $+ 8 \cdot 4$ m

   f) 6 m $+ 8$ m 25 cm

   g) 7 m 47 cm $+ 12$ m 93 cm

   h) 8 m $+ 888$ cm

   i) 7 m 45 cm $- 3$ m

   j) 6 m $- 4 \cdot 3$ m

   k) 850 cm $- 6$ m 60 cm

   l) 6 m 38 cm $- 4$ m

   m) 5 m $- 2 \cdot 75$ m

   n) 800 cm $- 4$ m 5 cm

4 Work out these.

   a) 4 kg $+ 300$ g

   b) $7 \cdot 3$ litres $+ 2 \cdot 5$ litres

   c) 850 g $+ 4455$ g (answer in kg)

   d) 6 kg $+ 500$ g

   e) $8 \cdot 7$ litres $+ 3 \cdot 6$ litres

   f) 300 g $+ 4545$ g (answer in kg)

   g) 8300 g $- 5$ kg

   h) $5 \cdot 67$ litres $- 2350$ ml

   i) $42 \cdot 60$ kg $- 17 \cdot 52$ kg

   j) 3550 g $- 1 \cdot 7$ kg

   k) $9 \cdot 05$ litres $- 3250$ ml

   l) $32 \cdot 96$ kg $- 9 \cdot 59$ kg

5 The sign on a canal tunnel states 'maximum height 2·40 m'.
Which of these barges could go through the tunnel and what would be the distances between the top of each barge and the roof of the tunnel?

a) height of barge = 1·95 m

b) height of barge = 2357 mm

c) height of barge = 236 cm

▌▌▐▌ EXERCISE 6.2H

Work out these.

1 a) 27 × 4 **b)** 52 × 7
  c) 48 × 9 **d)** 87 × 5
  e) 38 × 6

2 a) 34 × 50 **b)** 43 × 60
  c) 59 × 20 **d)** 28 × 90
  e) 93 × 40

3 a) 142 × 3 **b)** 265 × 4
  c) 137 × 5 **d)** 462 × 8
  e) 319 × 7

4 a) 4·7 × 6 **b)** 6·8 × 7
  c) 8·7 × 5 **d)** 5·6 × 5
  e) 5·9 × 8

STA

Working without a calculator

Work out these.

1 a) 25 × 17
b) 36 × 14
c) 57 × 12
d) 61 × 16
e) 82 × 21
f) 75 × 34
g) 28 × 43
h) 29 × 56
i) 47 × 82
j) 54 × 79

2 a) 7·45 × 4
b) 8·63 × 9
c) 4·75 × 6
d) 5·67 × 8
e) 6·59 × 7

3 a) 621 × 73
b) 487 × 39
c) 516 × 65
d) 926 × 48
e) 453 × 91

4 Jill has 15 shelves of books in her study.
Each shelf holds 24 books.
How many books are there in her study?

5 A seed tray holds 18 plants.
A nursery has 156 of these seed trays.
How many plants can they hold altogether?

Work out these.

1 a) 78 ÷ 6   **b)** 84 ÷ 3
   c) 95 ÷ 5   **d)** 28 ÷ 7
   e) 54 ÷ 9

2 a) 608 ÷ 8   **b)** 150 ÷ 6
   c) 225 ÷ 5   **d)** 976 ÷ 8
   e) 445 ÷ 5

3 a) 585 ÷ 13   **b)** 989 ÷ 23
   c) 928 ÷ 32   **d)** 986 ÷ 17
   e) 828 ÷ 36

4 a) 876 ÷ 17   **b)** 876 ÷ 27
   c) 860 ÷ 35   **d)** 980 ÷ 40
   e) 777 ÷ 26

5 423 people have booked to go on a special train
   excursion.
   Each carriage holds 56 people.
   How many carriages are needed?

6 In a cinema there are 828 seats.
   Each row has 36 seats.
   How many rows are there?

Writing formulae

EXERCISE 7.1H

In these questions, write down a formula using the letters given.

1 The total number of seats (s) in an assembly hall is found by multiplying the number of rows (r) by 20.

2 The perimeter (p) of a square is found by multiplying the length (l) of one side by 4.

3 The cost (c) of a child's bus fare is half of the cost (a) of an adult's bus fare.

4 Five friends divide a bag of sweets equally. To work out how many sweets each person (e) receives, divide the total number of sweets (s) by 5.

5 The time (t) needed, in minutes, to cook a piece of beef can be found by multiplying the weight (w) of the beef in kilograms by 40.

6 The area (a) of a rectangular room is found by multiplying the length (l) by the width (w).

7 The cost (£c) of hiring a car is a fixed charge of £30, plus £2 for each mile (m) travelled.

8 The cost, C pence, of x colas at y pence each.

9 The perimeter, P cm, of a regular hexagon of side x cm.

10 The number of grams of dried pasta, P, needed for n people, allowing 80 g per person.

11 A distance in kilometres, K, is the distance in miles, m, multiplied by 1·6.

12 The perimeter, P cm, of this rectangle in terms of w.

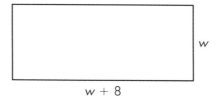

w

$w + 8$

STA

8 Angle properties

EXERCISE 8.1H pt

1 Find the sizes of these lettered angles.

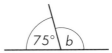

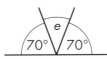

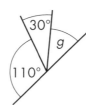

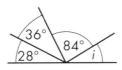

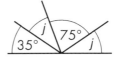

2 Find the sizes of these lettered angles.

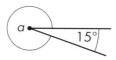

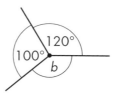

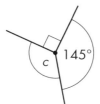

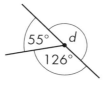

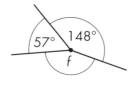

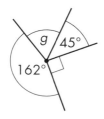

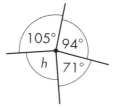

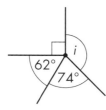

3 Find the size of each lettered angle.
Give a reason for each answer.

a)

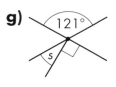

125° 55° b a

b)

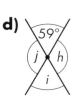

150° c 30° d

c)

137° f g e

d)

59° j h i

e)

82° m n k

f)

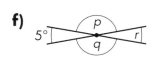

5° p r q

g)

121° s

h)

53° 37° v t u

i)

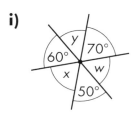

60° y 70° x w 50°

j)

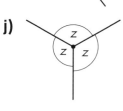

z z z

EXERCISE 8.2H

1 A triangle has two angles that are 84° and 45°.
Work out the size of the third angle.

2 An isosceles triangle has two angles that are 57°.
Work out the size of the third angle.

3 An isosceles triangle has an angle that is 76°.
Its other two angles are equal.
Work out the size of one of these angles.

4 Calculate the third angle in each of these triangles.

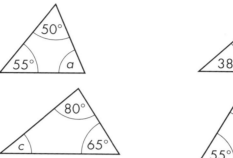

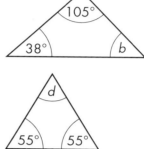

5 Work out the sizes of the angles in these diagrams.
Give reasons for your answers.

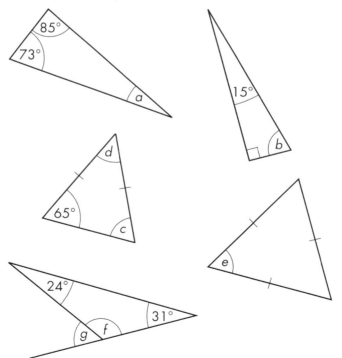

6 PQR is a triangle.
Angle QPR = 48° and angle PQR = 60°.
Sketch the triangle and find angle PRQ.

7 PQR is a triangle.
PRS is a straight line.
Angle QPR = 48° and angle PQR = 63°.

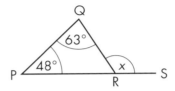

Calculate angle x.

8 ABCD is a rectangle.
P is halfway between B and C.

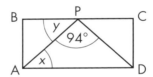

a) What type of triangle is APD?

b) Calculate the angles x and y.

9 In this diagram, LM and NP are straight lines.

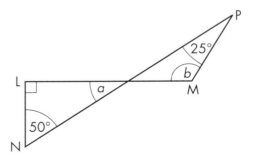

Calculate the size of angles a and b.

Reading from graphs

EXERCISE 9.1H

1 The line drawn on the graph is $y = 2 - 2x$.

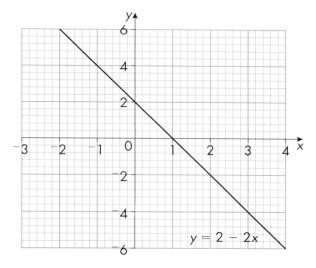

$$y = 2 - 2x$$

For the line,

a) find the value of y when
  (i) $x = 2$.
  (ii) $x = {}^-1$.

b) find the value of x when
  (i) $y = 0$.
  (ii) $y = {}^-6$.

STAG
4

2 The curve drawn on the graph is $y = x^2 - 4x$.

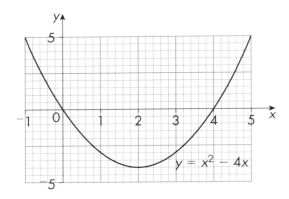

For the curve,

a) find the value of y when
   (i) $x = 3$.   **(ii)** $x = 5$.

b) find the value of x when
   (i) $y = {}^-4$.   **(ii)** $y = 0$.

3 Two graphs are drawn on the grid, $y = 20 - 3x^2$ and $y = 3x + 2$.

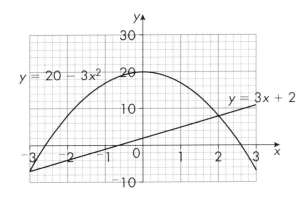

a) For the curve, find the value of y when
   (i) $x = 0$.   **(ii)** $x = {}^-1$.

b) Find the coordinates of the points where the line and the curve cross.

EXERCISE 9.2H

1 This graph shows Victoria's walk to her friend's house and back home.

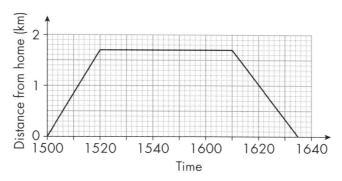

a) How far is it to Victoria's friend's house?

b) How long did she stay at her friend's house?

c) At what time did she get back home?

d) On which journey did she walk faster, going or coming back?

2 a) Draw a distance–time graph to show this cycle ride. Use a scale of 1 cm for 30 minutes and 1 cm for 5 km.

Robert left home at 9 a.m. and cycled 12 km in the next 45 minutes.
He then stopped for 15 minutes.
He continued his journey and went 10 km in the next 45 minutes.
After a half hour's break he cycled directly home, arriving there at 1 p.m.

b) Use your graph to answer these questions.
   (i)   How long did it take Robert to cycle back home?
   (ii) How far did he cycle altogether?
   (iii) What was his speed on the first section of his journey?

STAGE

4

3 Jenny and George both travelled on the same road from Guildford to Leicester.
This graph shows both their journeys.

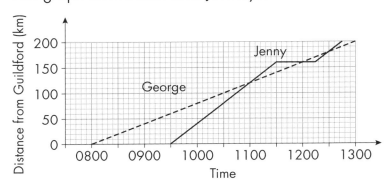

a) How much later than George did Jenny leave?

b) For how long did Jenny stop on the way?

c) What was George's average speed?

d) At what time did George and Jenny first pass each other?

e) How far were they from Guildford when they last passed each other?

4 A dog runs 100 metres in 20 seconds.

a) What is its speed in metres per second?

b) At this rate, how many kilometres would it run in 1 hour?

EXERCISE 9.3H

1 This graph shows Jack's charges for driving people to the airport.

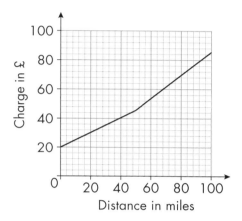

a) What does he charge for a journey of 40 miles?

b) For what distance in miles does he charge £62?

STA

2 This graph shows the number of ice creams Franco sold in the first week of July.

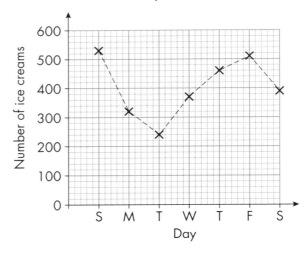

a) On which day did he sell the most ice creams?

b) How many more ice creams did he sell on Friday than on Saturday?

c) Why are the points joined with dashed lines instead of solid lines?

3 This graph shows the cost of two mobile phone plans for a month.

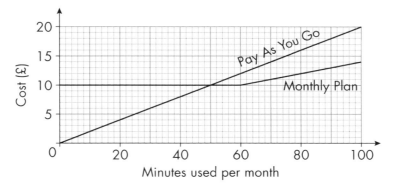

a) What is the cost of using 'Pay As You Go' for 20 minutes?

b) How many minutes do you get for £12 for each scheme?

c) Give two advantages of the 'Pay As You Go' scheme.

d) Give an advantage of the 'Monthly Plan' scheme.

STA

4 Online Banking produced this graph to support their claim that they pay 'more than double' the interest paid by Street Cash if you invest £5000 with them for 5 years.

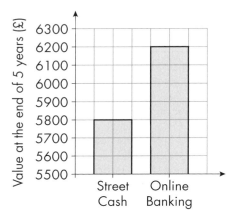

a) How much is the *interest* with Online Banking worth after 5 years?

b) How much is the *interest* with Street Cash worth after 5 years?

c) In what way is the graph misleading?

Factors, prime numbers and multiples

You may find the example useful for Exercises 10.1H and 10.2H.

EXERCISE 10.1H

1 Draw all the rectangular patterns for the number 30 that you can, and write down the product that each pattern shows.

2 Write down all the factors of these numbers.

a) 36

b) 49

c) 75

d) 80

e) 100

3 For the numbers 14, 18, 24, 25 and 60, find which has a factor of

a) 3.

b) 5.

c) 12.

d) both 6 and 8.

e) both 6 and 15.

4 Which of these numbers has 57 as a factor?
285   402   627   750   969

STAG
4

EXERCISE 10.2H

1 a) Find the factors of these numbers.
- **(i)** 12
- **(ii)** 18
- **(iii)** 36

b) Write down the common factors of 12, 18 and 36.

2 Find the common factors of 45 and 60.

3 Look at these numbers: 4, 12, 17, 21, 35.

a) Which have a factor of 2?

b) Which have a factor of 5?

c) Which have a factor of 3?

d) Which of these numbers are prime numbers?

4 Look at these numbers: 1, 2, 5, 15, 17, 18.
Write down the ones that are

a) multiples of 2.

b) factors of 50.

c) multiples of 3.

d) prime numbers.

5 Write down the common factors of

a) 24 and 45.

b) 15, 50 and 75.

c) 18 and 30.

6 Which of these numbers are prime numbers?
8, 13, 21, 23, 27, 33, 39, 43, 47, 49

EXERCISE 10.3H

1 Write down the first five multiples of each of these numbers.

a) 9   **b)** 16   **c)** 30   **d)** 22   **e)** 14

2 Find three common multiples of each of these sets of numbers.

a) 2 and 5

b) 3 and 7

c) 8 and 5

d) 9 and 4

e) 2, 5 and 9

3 Find two common multiples of each of these sets of numbers.

a) 2, 4 and 5

b) 2, 3 and 12

c) 4, 5, 6 and 15

d) 2, 5 and 15

e) 3, 7 and 9

4 Look at the numbers 35, 36, 43, 45, 56, 60, 61, 63. Write down which are

a) multiples of 2.

b) multiples of 3.

c) multiples of 5.

d) multiples of 7.

e) prime numbers.

11 The area of a rectangle

1 Find the area of these rectangles.
Give the units in your answer.

a)

2 cm

6 cm

b)

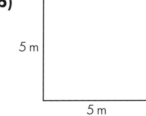

5 m

5 m

c)

3 mm

20 mm

d)

$\frac{1}{2}$ km

6 km

TAGE
4

90

2 A rectangle measures 5·3 cm by 2·6 cm.
Find its area.

3 A square has sides of length 3·6 cm.
Find its area.

4 A desk top is a rectangle measuring 1·2 m by 0·8 m.
Find its area.

5 The drive to a house is 3·5 m wide and 28 m long.

a) Work out the area of the drive.

b) The cost to tarmac the drive is £15 a square metre.
The cost to pave the drive is £27 a square metre.
How much is saved by having tarmac instead of paving?

6 The perimeter of a rectangle is 16·6 cm.
The shorter sides are 2·7 cm.
What is the area of the rectangle?

STA

12 Probability

EXERCISE 12.1H

1 Lizzie and Janna play tennis against each other each week.
Lizzie won 20 of their last 50 matches and Janna won 30.
Use these results to estimate the probability that Lizzie will win their match next week.

2 A fair six-sided dice is rolled 300 times. How many times would you expect to score

a) a 5?   **b)** an even number?

3 A newspaper headline says
'93% of 18-year-olds have a mobile phone'.
In a sixth form college there are one hundred and twenty 18-year-old students.
How many might be expected not to have a mobile phone?

4 Simon has a biased dice. He throws it 500 times and gets these results.

Number	1	2	3	4	5	6
Frequency	20	52	73	158	82	115

Use Simon's results to estimate the probability of getting a 4 with this dice.

5 Jo throws the same dice as Simon.
She throws it 50 times and gets 1 five times.
Explain how her result for throwing a 1 is different to Simon's and why this can happen.

EXERCISE 12.2H

1 A bag contains 20 balls.
There are 3 red, 12 blue, 1 yellow and 4 green balls.
One ball is chosen from the bag without looking.
What is the theoretical probability that it is blue?

2 When an ordinary dice is thrown, what is the
theoretical probability of getting

a) a 1?

b) a multiple of 3?

3 The arrow on this spinner is equally likely to land on
any of its eight sectors.

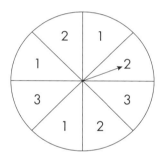

Jenny spun it 20 times and got these results.

Number on spinner	1	2	3
Number of times	10	6	4

a) Copy and complete this table.

Number on spinner	1	2	3
Theoretical probability			
Experimental probability			

b) Write one way in which Jenny's experimental
probabilities are different to the theoretical
probabilities.

4 Nikki spins an eight-sided spinner 200 times and records the number of times each score appears.

Number on spinner	Frequency
1	27
2	24
3	23
4	22
5	24
6	26
7	25
8	29

a) Do you think that Nikki's spinner is fair? Give a reason for your answer.

b) What is the probability that the next spin will show a 7?

5 Sunil made a spinner numbered 0, 1, 2, 3, 4 and he tested it 750 times.
The results are shown in this table.

Number on spinner	Frequency
0	187
1	149
2	236
3	78
4	100

a) Explain why Sunil's spinner is probably not fair.

b) Using this information, what is the probability that the next spin will show
(i) 0? **(ii)** an odd number?

AGE
4

Reflection

 **13**

For questions **1** to **5**, copy the shape and reflect it in the mirror line given.

1 Reflect the shape in the dashed line.

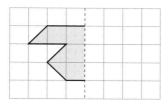

2 Reflect the shape in the dashed line.

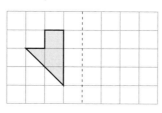

3 Reflect the shape in the dashed line.

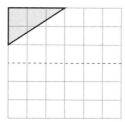

STAG

4

4 Reflect the shape in the dashed line.

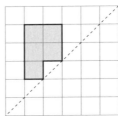

5 Reflect the shape in the *x*-axis.

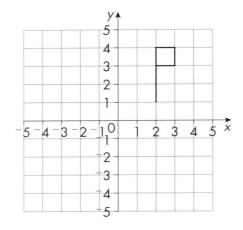

AGE
4

6 Draw axes from ⁻6 to 6 for both *x* and *y*.

   a) Plot the points (1, 1), (1, 3) and (4, 1) and join them to make a triangle. Label the triangle A.

   b) Plot the points P(⁻1, 6) and Q(⁻1, ⁻6). Join PQ.

   c) Reflect triangle A in the line PQ. Label the image B.

   d) Plot the points (1, ⁻1), (1, ⁻3) and (4, ⁻1) and join them to make a triangle. Label the triangle C.

   e) Describe the reflection that maps A on to C.

Ratio and proportion

EXERCISE 14.1H

1 To make a lime drink, lime cordial and water are mixed in the ratio 1 to 6.

a) How much water should be mixed with 30 ml of lime cordial?

b) How much lime cordial should be used with 450 ml of water?

2 A recipe for Banana Smoothie uses 400 g of banana puree for eight servings.
How much banana puree is needed to make Banana Smoothie for

a) 4 servings?

b) 12 servings?

c) 20 servings?

3 The length of a rectangle is twice as long as its width.

a) If the width of the rectangle is 12 cm, what is the length?

b) If the length of the rectangle is 10 cm, what is the width?

4 Kate is making concrete.
She mixes one bucket of cement with three buckets of sand.

a) How many buckets of sand does she need if she uses two buckets of cement?

b) How much cement does she need if she uses nine buckets of sand?

STAG
4

5 To make a potting mix, Simon uses four parts of loam to one part of compost.

a) If he uses 5 litres of compost, how much loam should he use?

b) If he uses 12 litres of loam
(i) how much compost does he need?
(ii) how much potting mix will he make?

6 A bread recipe uses one teaspoon of yeast to 500 g flour.

a) How much flour is needed for 3 teaspoons of yeast?

b) How much yeast is needed for 250 g flour?

7 A bar of brass contains 400 g of copper and 200 g of zinc.
Write the ratio of copper to zinc in its lowest terms.

8 A model of a theatre set is made on a scale of 1 to 20.

a) A rug on the set is 120 cm long.
How long is it on the model?

b) A cupboard on the model is 9 cm high.
How high is it on the set?

▌▐█ EXERCISE 14.2H

1 A recipe for raspberry flan for four people uses 200 g of raspberries.
What quantity of raspberries is needed in a flan for six people?

2 Anne and Jerry share the profits from their business in the ratio 3 to 2.

a) If Anne gets £6000, how much does Jerry get?

b) If Jerry gets £3000, how much does Anne get?

3 The width and length of a rectangle are in the ratio 2 to 5.

  a) If the width is 20 cm, what is the length?

  b) If the length is 60 cm, what is the width?

4 One picture is an enlargement of the other. What is the height of the larger picture?

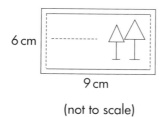

6 cm

9 cm

(not to scale)

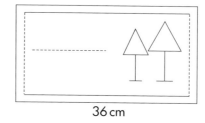

36 cm

5 The heights of Alice and her younger sister Karen are in the ratio 5 to 3.
Alice is 180 cm tall.
How tall is Karen?

6 Michael has a recipe for Twinkie Crackle that makes enough for eight people.
The recipe uses 200 g of Twinkies.

  a) What weight of Twinkies does Michael need to make enough Twinkie Crackle for six people?

  b) Michael has 325 g of Twinkies.
  How many people can he make Twinkie Crackle for?

7 In a local by-election, the number of votes was shared between the Liberal party and the Monster Raving Loony party in the ratio 19 : 2.
The Liberal party received 6289 votes.

  a) How many votes did the Monster Raving Loony party receive?

  b) How many votes were cast in the election?

15 Rotation symmetry

You may find the example useful
for both of these exercises.

EXERCISE 15.1H

1 Describe the rotation symmetry of these
letters.

a) Z   **b)** R

2 Write down the order of rotation symmetry
of each of these shapes.

a)
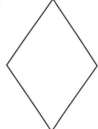

b)

c)

d)

e)

f)

g)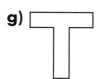

h)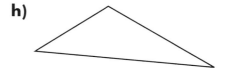

i)

j)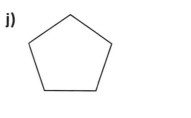

k)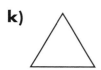

EXERCISE 15.2H

For each of these questions
- make a copy of the shape.
- draw in any lines of reflection symmetry.
- if there is rotation symmetry, show the centre and state the order of rotation symmetry.
- if there is no symmetry, say so.

1

2

3

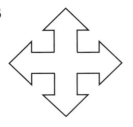

4

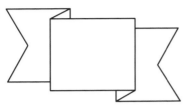

5

6

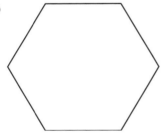

7

8

Solving problems 2

EXERCISE 16.1H

Use trial and improvement to solve these problems.

1 A number is multiplied by 4 and then 6 is added.
The result is 74.
Find the number.

2 A number is squared and 4 is subtracted.
The result is 117.
Find the number.

3 Pali is double Jill's age.
The sum of their ages is 57.
Find Jill's age.

4 The length of a rectangle is 5 cm more than the width.
The area is 204 cm^2.
Find the width of the rectangle.

5 The product of two consecutive numbers is 930.
Find the two numbers.

6 The sum of two consecutive odd numbers is 152.
Find the two numbers.

STAG
4

7 The length of a rectangle is 9 cm more than the width.
The perimeter of the rectangle is 50 cm.
Find the width of the rectangle.

8 Ken takes part in a race where he has to run and
cycle a total of 22 km.
Ken cycles three times the distance he runs.
How far does Ken have to run?

▌▌▌ EXERCISE 16.2H

Find these numbers by drawing the flow chart and
reversing it.

1 A number is multiplied by 4 and then 6 is added.
The result is 90.
Find the number.

2 A number is divided by 3, then 5 is subtracted.
The result is 17.
Find the number.

3 Mark thinks of a number, subtracts 2 and then
multiplies the answer by 5.
The result is 30.
What number did he think of?

4 A number is squared, then multiplied by 4, then 3 is
added.
The result is 147.
Find the number.

5 A number has 4 added to it, then the answer is
multiplied by 3 and then divided by 2.
The result is 39.
Find the number.

6 Mark thinks of a number, adds 48 and then divides
the answer by 5.
The result is 14.
What number did he think of?

7 A number is squared, then halved, then 8 is added.
The result is 80.
Find the number.

8 The sum of two consecutive numbers is squared.
The result is 361.
Find the two numbers.

STA

17 Metric and imperial measurements

EXERCISE 17.1H

1 In what imperial units would you give the mass of these?

a) A bag of sweets

b) Yourself

c) A pack of butter

2 In what metric units would you give the mass of these?

a) A bag of sweets

b) Yourself

c) A pack of butter

3 What metric units would you use to give these?

a) The area of a sheet of paper

b) The volume of a room

c) The area of Yorkshire

4 In what metric units would you give the capacity of these?

a) A bath

b) A carton of milk

c) A large pond

5 Which of these is closest to the area of a sheet of A4 paper?

$6000 \, mm^2$ $0.6 \, m^2$ $600 \, cm^2$ $0.06 \, cm^2$

6 A medicine bottle holds 240 ml and contains enough for 16 doses.
Choose the most likely of these measurements for the size of a single dose.

1500 ml   0·15 litres   150 cl   15 ml

EXERCISE 17.2H

Use a calculator if you wish but only give rough or approximate answers.

1 Change these from imperial units to their rough metric equivalents.

a) 10 feet   **b)** 2 inches   **c)** 100 miles

d) 100 lb   **e)** 2 lb   **f)** 14 lb

g) 28 pints   **h)** 4 gallons   **i)** 7 gallons

2 Change these from metric units to their rough imperial equivalents.

a) 900 cm   **b)** 25 km   **c)** 3 m

d) 90 kg   **e)** 6 kg   **f)** 500 g

g) 36 litres   **h)** 6 litres   **i)** 16 litres

3 James is 179 cm tall.
What is his approximate height in feet and inches?

4 Pat drives 25 km to get to work each day, and also drives home.
She works every day from Monday to Friday.
Approximately how many miles does Pat drive each week?

5 A particular type of string can be bought in 500-foot or 150-metre balls.
The balls of string cost £9·49 each.
Which ball is the best value for money?

6 A large tank is used to fill two troughs with water at the same time.
Water flows into each trough at the same rate.
Which trough will fill first, one that holds 100 gallons or one that holds 500 litres?